W9-AXU-745

Praise for *Smart Communities*

"*Smart Communities* reminds us that nurturing community is the most difficult, most daunting, and most important work we do. Morse challenges us to get this right, and thankfully she leads the way."
—**Sherry Magill**, president, Jessie Ball duPont Fund

"Any community members looking to move beyond that which has defined them for years, into a thriving community, owe it to themselves to read this book. Morse provides not only powerful tools for a community's resurgence, but also insightful examples of how community leaders and citizens alike sought to remake their communities and succeeded. I was so taken by its timeless and compelling strategies that I bought 50 copies and handed them out around town."
—**Daniel J. Phelan**, president, Jackson College, Michigan

"With *Smart Communities,* Suzanne Morse has achieved a unique blend of a national perspective and a community-centered study of what has helped, and will help, communities be successful over the long haul. There are many valuable lessons to be learned here, none more essential—whether for a big urban city or a small rural town—than preserving and maximizing assets. Communities that make best use of their assets will win, and Morse gives us all a road map for getting there."
—**Anne B. Pope**, executive director, Tennessee Commission for the Arts, and former federal cochair, Appalachian Regional Commission

"A strong nation is dependent on strong communities—people coming together to address the problems of the community and its members. *Smart Communities* addresses how we can work together to help strengthen our nation."
—**Alma Powell**, chair, America's Promise Alliance

"Suzanne Morse's *Smart Communities* is an inspirational, informative road map for all those who want to tackle public problems and strengthen their communities. There should be a copy in every public library. Read it, take hope from it, and use it!"
—**Martha McCoy**, executive director, Everyday Democracy, and president, The Paul J. Aicher Foundation

Join Us at
Josseybass.com
▼

JOSSEY-BASS™
An Imprint of
Ⓦ**WILEY**

Register at **www.josseybass.com/email**
for more information on our publications,
authors, and to receive special offers.

The Instructor's Guide to accompany
the second edition of *Smart Communities*
is available for free at
www.wiley.com/college/morse

SMART COMMUNITIES

How Citizens and Local Leaders Can Use Strategic Thinking to Build a Brighter Future

Second Edition

Suzanne W. Morse

JB JOSSEY-BASS™
A Wiley Brand

Cover design by Michael Cook
Cover image © iStockphoto

Copyright © 2014 by John Wiley & Sons, Inc. All rights reserved.

Published by Jossey-Bass
A Wiley Brand
One Montgomery Street, Suite 1200, San Francisco, CA 94104-4594—www.josseybass.com

No part of this publication may be reproduced, stored in a retrieval system, or transmitted in any form or by any means, electronic, mechanical, photocopying, recording, scanning, or otherwise, except as permitted under Section 107 or 108 of the 1976 United States Copyright Act, without either the prior written permission of the publisher, or authorization through payment of the appropriate per-copy fee to the Copyright Clearance Center, Inc., 222 Rosewood Drive, Danvers, MA 01923, 978-750-8400, fax 978-646-8600, or on the Web at www.copyright.com. Requests to the publisher for permission should be addressed to the Permissions Department, John Wiley & Sons, Inc., 111 River Street, Hoboken, NJ 07030, 201-748-6011, fax 201-748-6008, or online at www.wiley .com/go/permissions.

Limit of Liability/Disclaimer of Warranty: While the publisher and author have used their best efforts in preparing this book, they make no representations or warranties with respect to the accuracy or completeness of the contents of this book and specifically disclaim any implied warranties of merchantability or fitness for a particular purpose. No warranty may be created or extended by sales representatives or written sales materials. The advice and strategies contained herein may not be suitable for your situation. You should consult with a professional where appropriate. Neither the publisher nor author shall be liable for any loss of profit or any other commercial damages, including but not limited to special, incidental, consequential, or other damages. Readers should be aware that Internet Web sites offered as citations and/or sources for further information may have changed or disappeared between the time this was written and when it is read.

Jossey-Bass books and products are available through most bookstores. To contact Jossey-Bass directly call our Customer Care Department within the U.S. at 800-956-7739, outside the U.S. at 317-572-3986, or fax 317-572-4002.

Wiley publishes in a variety of print and electronic formats and by print-on-demand. Some material included with standard print versions of this book may not be included in e-books or in print-on-demand. If this book refers to media such as a CD or DVD that is not included in the version you purchased, you may download this material at http://booksupport.wiley.com. For more information about Wiley products, visit www.wiley.com.

Library of Congress Cataloging-in-Publication Data
Morse, Suzanne W. (Suzanne Whitlock)
  Smart communities : how citizens and local leaders can use strategic thinking to build a brighter future / Suzanne W. Morse. —Second edition.
    pages cm
  Includes bibliographical references and index.
  ISBN 978-1-118-42700-2 (cloth); ISBN 978-1-118-84357-4 (ebk); ISBN 978-1-118-84355-0 (ebk)
1. Community leadership. 2. Community organization. I. Title.
  HM781.M67 2014
  307—dc23
                            2013046336

Printed in the United States of America
SECOND EDITION
HB Printing 10 9 8 7 6 5 4 3 2 1

Contents

Preface

Ten years ago the world had not talked on an iPhone; communicated via YouTube, Twitter, or Facebook; learned the ins and outs of organizational politics from characters on *The Office*; or seen the nation's talent on *American Idol*. Three-dimensional printers now are making artificial limbs more compatible; dental crowns, implants, and dentures more affordable; and the prospects for new applications unlimited. No one would argue that enormous technological and social changes have not occurred during the past decade.

Unfortunately, far too much has not changed. Rates of poverty hover at the 15 percent mark, and too many Americans barely make ends meet, if at all. The world watched while Hurricane Katrina exposed our national inequities through the lens of New Orleans; Detroit and Kodak went bankrupt; and Youngstown shrank. The culprit for the downward spiral is not one thing or one program or even the Great Recession of 2007–2009, but a concentration of systemic issues. In this cloud of dust, however, places such as Houston grew, an auto trail in the South was forged, and regions such as the Fox Cities showed how it is done. Research over the last fifty years says that if policies, practices, programs, and the public will could align, the numbers would improve and self-sufficiency would increase. A clear definition of the problems and challenges, an openness to opportunities, and an implementation strategy for the long run are needed to make real change. The secret formula is merging how to work with precise community priorities.

With so much of our lives going online, day-to-day interactions have taken a hit. However, in our bigger, better, faster world of the twenty-first century, some fundamental requirements hold firm.

We need relationships in our lives, we need places for restoration and regeneration, and we need community. The editor-in-chief of *Popular Mechanics* magazine, James Meigs, said this: "Just because high-tech change is possible doesn't mean we always want it," citing the recent craft, natural fabrics, and slow food movements as evidence (July 24, 2013). Community work past, present, and future really is about keeping what works, losing what doesn't, and inventing new approaches. Sociologist David Reisman said, "America is a land of second chances" (Potter, 1996, p. viii). The ideas presented in this book give every community in America a fresh start.

What communities need in order to embrace the changing global world with confidence is to take a holistic approach to success—not one thing but many—and to base their collective decisions on three critical factors: 1) the most objective and precise information available to fit their size, geographic location, and circumstances; 2) a collective vision of where they want to go; and 3) a collaborative strategy for achieving that vision. Success will not happen without all three. The challenges that communities face in achieving these three objectives can be summed up by Yogi Berra's (1998) comment to his wife on a long and circuitous trip to the Baseball Hall of Fame in Cooperstown, New York: "We are completely lost, but we are making good time." Yogi's optimism notwithstanding, he spoke volumes about the way that too many community members and elected officials approach the future: just keep driving in the same direction and maybe we will get there. That strategy has never worked and never will!

The Ideas That Inform This Book

Communities across the world face an array of challenges, not the least of which is the moving target of the world economy. While a range of ecological and social problems need to be solved, perhaps the most pressing dilemma for places of all sizes is how to make gains in the changing economy while preserving a strong quality of life. Some would say we want it all—and we do. We want to make a living wage and have choices about where we live and how.

The first edition of *Smart Communities* was supported by powerful examples of places that were defying the odds on a range of issues based on their ability to work in different ways. It was clear from that early research that the communities which were doing the best had less division about direction, more engagement from community members, and an enlarged vision of what could be. In place after place, we saw sparkplugs that generated a new future. In Tupelo, Mississippi, newspaper publisher George McLean ignited the future more than eighty years ago. In western North Carolina, a small group believed that the region's rich tradition of arts and crafts could be the change that was needed. Or in Fargo, North Dakota, and Moorhead, Minnesota, demographic changes fueled new and unexpected opportunities to work together. The list goes on. We were certain ten years ago, and we are certain now, that sustainable change requires new ways of working. But there is another step in the process: action. That action begins by using community resources, stakeholders, and assets to craft a new vision and then defining and implementing a strategy to reach that vision. Recently, I was in a very small community trying to find the most direct route to a town in the same region. When I stopped a passerby to ask directions, he replied, "There are many ways to get there from here." When I said just give me one, he said, "Where are you starting from?" Well, we are starting from here with the belief that implementing the seven strategies of *Smart Communities* will get you to your destination in a timely way:

- Invest right the first time
- Work together
- Build on community strengths
- Practice democracy
- Preserve the past
- Grow new leaders
- Invent a brighter future

An additional ten years of civic practice and research has affirmed that process + action is the gold standard formula for success.

Finding a Guide for Success: Process + Action

The Pew Partnership for Civic Change and its successor organization, Civic Change, Inc., worked with over one hundred communities in a twenty-year span on a range of issues. We began this work in 1992 focused on smaller cities; over the years that research expanded to include some of the largest. As report after report was crafted, the same observations seemed to hold no matter the place or the evaluator. One of the first reports on the findings of the fourteen original Pew Partnership communities, *Just Call It Effective*, identified eight characteristics of change strategies that were working in those cities: 1) had more players at the table; 2) involved new people who built new relationships; 3) built collaboration and partnerships; 4) worked and thought long-term; 5) addressed significant issues and values; 6) took responsibility for the change that they wanted; 7) invented the strategies that worked for that place at that time; and 8) balanced their approach and emphasis (Dewar, Dodson, Paget, and Roberts, 1998). Fifteen years later, another report, *What Makes a Solution*, had complementary findings: 1) long-term commitment to the most pressing programs is critical; 2) collaboration is key; 3) an ounce of prevention goes a long way; 4) research counts to raise public awareness, build support, and expand coalitions; 5) focus is usually on a unit of measurement—families, neighborhoods, and whole communities (Freedman, 2003). These findings and conversations with literally thousands of community members, local policymakers, and researchers helped shaped the seven leverage points that comprise the *Smart Communities* process. Although the issues were different across the communities evaluated in these two reports, the ways of working were not.

The *Smart Communities* framework provides an everyday strategy for community members, policymakers, and civic leaders to actually change the future. Applying the seven leverage points produces better decisions, builds a stronger sense of community and inclusion for all who live there, and is the strongest line of defense against globalization, budget cuts, and a changing economy.

As community after community has used the framework to reorder and remake its civic work culture, the inevitable question arises: now what? Once the seven points are fully embraced, the next step is to apply the new way of working to an issue-based agenda. Based on that question, we developed a data-driven model, The Thriving Communities Model®, to test out two important questions: Where should communities invest? Do quality-of-life investments impact a thriving economy? Using multiple regression techniques, we analyzed economic and quality-of-life variables in 358 metropolitan statistical areas to determine the answers. The analysis showed that a vibrant economy creates a high quality of life and that a high quality of life creates a thriving economy. Neither element was more important than the other, and both must be present for communities to be successful. A strong economy leads to a robust quality of life as much as a robust quality of life leads to a strong economy. This finding cements what community development professionals and community members have argued for years—place still matters.

The Thriving Communities Model defined a successful community as one where employment, per-capita income, median household income, and poverty all beat the national averages. A robust quality of life was defined as a first-rate educational system, lower taxes, affordable housing, access to health care, a strong emphasis on the arts and plentiful recreation, transportation connections, a low crime rate, and high social capital. Using the correlation of these factors between and among each other, a pattern emerged of the strongest cities in each category. The collective analysis of all 358 communities and the lessons learned from them are the foundation of the best practices and insights discussed in this book. Building a strong economy and high quality of life lead to a competitive advantage that can impact all areas of a community. This requires that communities be nimble, adaptable to new circumstances, and innovative in their approaches. This research shows communities how to merge process with practice with better results. However, the process is not complex or the practices mysterious. They are commonsense.

As Denise Shekerjian (1990) reminds us in her book on creative genius, much of what is needed in life is hard work, determination, and resolve:

> It's far preferable to believe in thunderbolts than it is to have to face up to the mundane, trivial workaday world. It might come as a disappointment, then, to realize that behind any creative piece of work is a lot of earthbound effort, part of which is concerned with the conscious arrangements of conditions suitable for encouraging one's creative impulses. (pp. 44–45)

Who Should Read This Book and Why

Smart Communities differs from other community-building books in key ways. First, it embeds process into results. Not only does it highlight successes, but it also discusses the process needed to attain them.

Second, the book has a foundation that includes theory, practice-based research, and quantitative and qualitative data. This multifaceted approach leads to a better understanding of how community problem solving can lead to success. The research that grounds *Smart Communities* is not guesswork. The discussion of each of the seven leverage points includes both foundational research and illustrations of successful community applications.

Third, the book moves out of midsize-to-large cities and examines practices and results in smaller cities, towns, and rural areas. Jane Jacobs (1961) cautioned that we cannot extrapolate what we learn from small cities and towns to what she calls the Great Cities, but I think we can. Small-to-midsize cities and towns can be laboratories for the change that is needed. Scale allows a more precise investigation. In other words, this book identifies the kinds of practices that will work anywhere.

Smart Communities is for all those people who have a say—or want a say—in the decisions affecting their community. The ideas will have more impact when they are taken as a whole. While each principle stands alone, all are necessary to achieve success. Further, the strategies will be most effective if they are understood and practiced by more than just a few people. They can prompt a communitywide conversation about what is working and what needs to be changed. To be smart, communities must act smart. That requires new thinking and more action—together. The lessons of the book can be instructive to several key audiences: newly elected or appointed officials, business and nonprofit leaders, community-based researchers, community members and civic leaders, college and university faculty and students, and local and national funders.

Elected or appointed officials are under increased pressure to produce results while not raising taxes. While they may know intellectually what needs to be done, they lack the examples or best cases to sell their approach to the public, particularly if public funds are involved. Corporate leaders, development directors, and chambers of commerce know well that quality of life is the tipping point for business location, relocation, and expansion. Yet too often the emphasis is only on economic incentives and one-industry solutions.

For community researchers, the book provides new places to look for best practices and new variables to consider as community success is evaluated. It points the spotlight on a way of working that creates both the foundation for and the likelihood of successful outcomes.

In academia, schools and departments of urban and regional planning, sociology, public administration, and policy have tended to focus attention and study in community development courses on federal and state policy rather than on community practice and validated research. It is critical that students understand what is required of them "on the ground" to make progress on issues as they begin their careers or continue their studies. Students from a variety of disciplines will see in real time the importance of inclusive planning and engagement, timely investments, asset-based development, and the role that elected officials and public administrators can and should play. This book will give students a new lens and new tools for analyzing community success and process for their research, course work, and service learning.

For service learning and engagement professionals, this book provides students with the skills and the processes that they will need in their community placements and research. This book takes the reader behind the scenes to a better understanding of how communities actually can work.

For community members and civic leaders, this book is intended to provide direction but also to be a blueprint for what must be done and could be done. If there is a place or section in the book where you say, "My community could never do that," then get started to create the will and opportunity for it to happen.

Local and national funders will find both a template and a map in this research for their own work. The leverage points offer a way of working that can be fostered by investing in the capacity of community members and local and regional organizations to learn and apply these principles. In some ways, it is validation for the work already being done or on the drawing board. The case examples show the possible. For every community that thinks it "can't," someplace else assumes it can. The questions for funders are how to be more efficient with funding and how to be more effective with all available resources.

Finally, this book presents a new approach to determining community advantage in the globalized world by focusing on the interrelationship of economic prosperity, quality of life, and place using tested practices of change. The individuals, organizations, and communities profiled in this book addressed the problem, whatever it was, and took action. They did not gloss over it, wring their hands, or play the blame game. They took responsibility and made smart decisions. They listened. They worked together. They kept at it until the job was done. They found new routes to address old problems.

Identifying the Cases

We used a variety of scans in the community selection. We examined lists of all kinds and also national databases such as The Annie E. Casey Foundation KIDS COUNT® (2013), the Thriving Communities data set, and the U.S. Census. But most important, we visited many of the cities for ourselves. We were not looking for perfect communities, but rather those that were applying the leverage points in real-time. Like ten years ago, some cities are considered "hot." These are the go-to places of what works, such as Austin, both Portlands, and Chattanooga. You will see these cities profiled here, but you also will see "outliers." These are new places that you may not have thought about much, which are doing really interesting things in innovative ways.

But all of the communities profiled will tell you that none of this is easy at first or even down the way. As one community leader told me, "We are really making progress, but some days it is really frustrating." Indeed, that is what community work can be: frustrating, rewarding, and hard work. As communities go about implementing the seven leverage points, the process can be messy, all over the board, and incredibly frustrating. But when that happens, add some new people to the work, get out the map, and keep all eyes focused on the vision. This book gives some instructions on how to do all three.

Overview of Contents

Chapter One, "Building the Foundation for Community Change," provides a brief discussion of how cities have evolved and why. This includes the impact of key public policies, the advent of the global economy, and the changes in demographics and location preferences.

Chapter Two, "Investing Right the First Time," develops the idea that communities need investment strategies which allow them to prevent problems rather than just react to them. Communities have a wide array of capital to bring to issues and opportunities. Many of these issues are referred to as "wicked" problems. The challenge is to identify strategic ways to use capital for the strongest results in addressing these problems. This chapter also introduces the concept of Triple Bottom Line budgeting, investing, and decision making for communities. Cases profiled are Minneapolis, Minnesota; Ann Arbor, Michigan; Portland, Oregon; and Seattle, Washington—all communities with strong investment results.

Chapter Three, "Working Together," examines the advantages and the practicality of community members and adjacent communities working together. In a world of fences, barriers, and divisions, the smartest communities are finding ways to work together across fault lines and county lines. The chapter discusses vehicles that communities can use to organize themselves for more collaborative approaches and overcome the barriers that prevent them. Through the case examples of Chattanooga, Tennessee; Almena, Wisconsin; and Austin, Texas, the principles, practices, and value of new ways of working are illustrated.

Chapter Four, "Building on Community Strengths," illustrates how ways of new thinking can lead to better results. Twenty years ago two Northwestern University researchers put forth an idea that communities have undiscovered assets that could be brought to bear on old problems and new opportunities. Emphasizing assets over deficits can change minds and outcomes for those inside communities and can change the lens for those outside. The asset-based approach to development unleashes possibilities for change. Four communities illustrate how looking within with new eyes and perspectives can make all the difference: the

Broadmoor Neighborhood in New Orleans; Chimney Rock, North Carolina; and two Texas cities, Saluda and Hidalgo.

Chapter Five, "Practicing Democracy," examines new ways of engaging and participating in politics as well as some time-tested engagement methods. As the world has become more linked electronically, the inevitable question is whether we are more engaged or not. This chapter looks at whether technology can be a key factor in stronger democratic practice and, if so, how that can happen. Dialogue, public deliberation, and engagement are not luxuries in a democracy; they are necessary components for sustained action.

All three of the engagement formats profiled—Oregon Citizens' Initiative Review, Jacksonville Community Council, Inc., and Hampton, Virginia, city government—are instructive on ways that new media, old media, and participatory democracy can work together.

Chapter Six, "Preserving the Past," examines how communities are using buildings, culture, and history to create different scenarios for the future that contribute greatly to the economic and quality-of-life indices. Cultural stories and historic places bind communities together and allow new perspectives and ideas to emerge. More and more places are turning inward as they look for levers to position their community in the global economy. In different ways, each of the community initiatives profiled has led to goals that improve the overall well-being of the community and its members by building on the past. The designation of historic places, the restoration of important buildings, and the rejuvenation of the downtown all have given Lowell, Massachusetts; Birmingham, Alabama; Charlottesville, Virginia; Denver, Colorado; and Asheville, North Carolina, new life, new possibilities, and new revenue.

Chapter Seven, "Growing New Leaders," looks at the broadbased, strategic leadership that is needed to create a thriving economy and a strong quality of life. Communities are filled with people—community champions—who do and could make significant contributions to conversations and strategies needed to implement change. Too often, the same people direct the conversation and the agenda. The new metaphor for community leadership is bench strength—getting people prepared, activated, and encouraged to get involved. This chapter presents profiles on three community champions—from Charleston, South Carolina; Harlem in New York City; and Tupelo, Mississippi—whose example shows how one person can make a difference. There are also examples of two organizations, the Kansas Health Foundation and the Northwest Area Foundation, with different missions and purposes, which have identified leadership bench strength as a key strategy for addressing "wicked" problems.

Chapter Eight, "Inventing the Future," looks at what it takes to create a new future. Just as innovators and inventors need to find new ways to make things easier, faster, and more accessible and sustainable, so do communities. Communities faced with new realities have learned that old ways of working and investing are not producing the needed results; they are inventing new futures. The examples of Pittsburgh, Pennsylvania; Grand Rapids, Michigan; Greenville-Spartanburg, South Carolina; and Cumberland, Maryland, show how communities have built on their past, invested in their future, and used the principles that make smarter communities.

Sir Winston Churchill once said, "Doing your best is sometimes not enough; you have to do what is required." The future of our communities rests on our ability to take action together to create futures that build a strong economy and a high quality of life for all and with all.

As the following chapters illustrate, success is neither place nor size bound. It comes from a set of seven tested leverage points that help all communities decide their futures. Based on ten years of additional observation and research, these seven principles are still the "north star" for community work.

Charlottesville, Virginia   Suzanne Morse
February 2014

Acknowledgments

Having the chance to revisit the ideas and places of *Smart Communities* a decade later is a privilege and an honor. Tremendous work is happening in every corner of the country. I have seen it for myself. Since the first writing, I have visited many communities and regions that are determined to get things done right. The times demand new thinking and action, and plenty of places are doing just that. While this edition contains new ideas and new illustrations, the fundamental belief that communities can be stronger and better if they work differently remains steadfast. As I revisited the communities profiled ten years ago, I was inspired when I heard about their successes. Perhaps the biggest difference between this version of the book and the original is the mounting evidence that these principles are working to make communities thrive.

I want to thank the many people who took the time to talk with me about their communities and introduced me to the people and processes that are behind their success. Community members spoke with pride and hope, but also realism, about the work completed and still to be done. I have learned from them to stay the course but change when needed, look around for good ideas and examples to borrow from and adapt, and plan for change.

My appreciation goes to the reviewers, whose advice and suggestions were critical in reshaping this edition, and especially to Alison Hankey, senior editor at Jossey-Bass/Wiley, who convinced me that the ten-year edition not only was needed but also was a really good idea. Her encouragement has been the foundation of the writing process.

Thanks also go to all the people who supported the effort this time and also the first time around, including the Pew Partnership for Civic Change networks and my colleagues at The Pew Charitable Trusts. For this second edition, faculty and students at the University of Virginia, School of Architecture, have been great supporters and advisers on this work. Dean Kim Tanzer's financial support allowed for a summer of uninterrupted writing and the assistance of a research team. That team included Harriett Jameson, my principal researcher for two years, as well as a great group who joined her at different points in the process: Alexander Kaplan, Lucas Lyons, Kate Murtagh, Julia Triman, and Thomas Wheet. Thank you all for your first-rate research assistance and for your great ideas and insights into the cases and their implications. Also, a word of thanks goes to the Jossey-Bass editorial teams for their skill and care in seeing the book through the process.

Finally, my son, Will, who is one of those future leaders whom any community would be glad to welcome, was a great source of inspiration. My sincerest appreciation goes to him and to our family and friends, who have been patient, supportive, encouraging, and indulgent regarding my late arrivals and early departures. And last but not least, this edition is dedicated to Ned, whose wisdom about these matters was unparalleled and whose support was unfailing.

—S.W.M.

The Author

Specializing in community and economic development at the local, national, and international levels, **Suzanne W. Morse** leads a distinguished career in the nonprofit and philanthropic worlds as well as in academia. She is associate professor of urban and regional planning in the School of Architecture at the University of Virginia, director of the Community Design and Research Center at UVA, and academic lead of the Appalachian Prosperity Project. In 1992 she was the founding president and chief executive officer of Civic Change, Inc. (formerly Pew Partnership for Civic Change).

Founder of the national dropout initiative Learning to Finish®, Morse is a national commentator on issues facing cities and regions worldwide. She chairs the board of trustees of the Kettering Foundation and was the chair of the Piedmont Virginia Community College Board from 2010 to 2012. She has served on several national boards, including Campfire, Inc., LBJ School of Public Affairs, and the Constitutional Studies Committee at Montpelier. She has been a fellow at the Virginia Foundation for the Humanities and the Institute for Advanced Learning and Research at Virginia Tech. In 2002 she received the Ethical Leadership Award from the Content of Our Character Project at Duke University. Morse holds a Ph.D. from The University of Alabama. She lives in Charlottesville, Virginia.

SMART COMMUNITIES

CHAPTER ONE

Building the Foundation for Community Change

In a wonderful anecdote told by Gerald Taylor of the Industrial Areas Foundation, we begin to understand what this idea of change really means. The "Accident Ministry" was an outreach program for a rural church located at the end of a winding road. As traffic increased just before services and with little signage, the number of accidents began to increase. The congregation saw this as an opportunity to minister and administer to the affected parishioners. But as the ministry grew and volunteers became concerned about keeping up with the demand, the future of the Accident Ministry was in question. A meeting after services to discuss the problem generated this suggestion, "Why don't we just straighten the road?"

For too many of us a direct route to anything seems too hard. It is expensive, time consuming, and a little boring just to do what needs to be done. The glitz and rush of a new project or initiative excites people, builds hope, and creates a sense of possibility. What these efforts are less likely to do is show the whole scenario, all that it would take to really straighten the road and get the signs going in the right direction. This book and the seven leverage points proposed here are about the long haul. They provide a way for communities no matter their location, circumstances, or size to create change for better results. The book should stimulate a new conversation in a community, giving community members of all ages a different lens on the change that is needed, and provide a road map of sorts for developing the strategy to make it happen.

Knowing Where to Build the Road

Over the last few decades, there has been an increase in the "Top Ten" lists for communities. The music industry has benefited from the popular appeal of these lists for music buyers and radio airtime for many years. Getting on the list meant exposure and sales. Not surprisingly, the media and communities alike have been drawn into the plethora of community ratings that focus on a particular demographic group like the "best places to raise children" or the "best places to retire"—a pecking order of who's best on a range of criteria. Touted by local boosters as proof that one community or region is better than another, the rankings may be a point of local pride but they are only snapshots. They are not particularly helpful for directing an action agenda or understanding the threats and opportunities that a community may face. Community change requires new ways of thinking and acting. Citizens in each of the communities discussed here, and hundreds like them, have ideas—good ideas—that need to be understood, tailored, communicated, and acted upon. However, among this variegated landscape that we call community, there are no perfect ones. Even those with elaborate fountains, revitalized Main Streets, and robust economies still have issues to address.

In *Change by Design*, Tim Brown (2009) observes that there is not just one way to solve problems. He describes the nonlinear continuum of the innovation process around a system of steps that are iterative and circular. First, the *Inspiration* portion of the process defines the problem and the opportunity to be addressed. Second, the *Ideation* stage is the process of generating and testing ideas. And the third stage, *Implementation*, takes ideas to market and generates action. He argues that this is not a disorganized approach but rather allows for the kind of exploration that leads to new discoveries. This kind of fluid approach is difficult for some groups to handle. Times are so tough and demands so immediate that giving new ideas time to gel is counterintuitive. Too many of us want answers now; waiting for the long haul or not seeing immediate results is hard and frustrating.

The issues that concern us most in our communities are those "wicked" problems such as educational attainment, poverty, environmental degradation, and social and economic inequities.

These problems were not created overnight and thus the "fix" will take time as well. What we see now is the cumulative effect of our inability to act and invest, not for a few years, but for generations. Solutions, while possible, will require hard work, more investments, and smarter ways to work. No quick fix or computer software will do it. It will demand skills, talents, and people that we haven't tapped.

How We Got Where We Are

As new ways of working are crafted, the context of the history of urban development and its modern-day implications brings a helpful perspective. Community members and policymakers often want the tested research, development, and implementation strategies that stay in straight lines and produce the expected results. Good luck with that! Communities are not programmable or predictable. They are embedded in systems and environments that act and react in different ways. Change of any kind works that way.

As communities and citizens look to one another for answers to the most compelling social questions of our time, they must look deep and wide. American communities range from Almena, Wisconsin (population 677), to Tupelo, Mississippi (34,546), to Portland, Oregon (583,776), to New York City (8.175 million) (U.S. Bureau of the Census, 2010). The more than 311 million people who reside in America live in communities of all sizes and descriptions. Within this broad spectrum, all places share promise and peril. Extraordinarily poor people live on rural farms and in high-rise apartments. Economic downturns hit cities, suburbs, and small towns without favor. Although the nation's urban policy has never directed America's population to be spread among places of all sizes, that is exactly what has happened. Even with rural areas shrinking and cities expanding, America still has a variety of place and location. Suburbs are no longer just inner ring or outer ring. They respond to the central city and one another in unique ways and become cities themselves. Rural areas abut major metropolitan areas and are accessible to them by a short car or train ride or connect via broadband to the world. Small cities connect to other small cities to create regional presence.

Some of the early American cities that started strong have faltered; new places have sprung up seemingly overnight. In a 2013 analysis of the cities that have grown the fastest since the 2007–2009 Great Recession began, almost all are in the Deep South, the Intermountain West, and the suburbs of larger cities (Kotkin, 2013). Chula Vista, California, is one of those former suburbs now termed a "new city." Once a suburb of San Diego, its population has grown almost 22 percent in the last decade. Likewise, Carmel, Indiana, is another example of the growth and evolution of suburban cities. Thirty-five years ago its primary role as a bedroom community began to change. Now the City of Carmel is home to over eighty-one thousand people, a 62 percent increase since 2004. It is a great place to live in part because of some key investments in quality of life. Carmel's metamorphosis happened because of its geographic proximity to Indianapolis, surely, but also because the area's leadership has attracted major employers and invested in quality-of-life attributes such as the arts, downtown redevelopment, and a nationally recognized public library.

Jefferson, Texas, in contrast, was the "Riverport to the Southwest" in the mid-nineteenth century, a bustling port where Mississippi River cargo boats loaded and unloaded. In a time before the railroads came to north Texas, Jefferson provided the only alternative for importing and exporting for the region. In its heyday, Jefferson was second only to Galveston in cargo tonnage shipped from Texas. Jefferson's decline was prompted in part by a decision taken by the U.S. Corps of Engineers in 1873 to remove a natural barrier on the Red River called the Great Raft, which dropped the water level in the port so that shipping was questionable and no longer profitable. The coming of the railroads completed the demise. Today, Jefferson is a quaint town that has built a premier tourist industry around the river and its prestigious past (City of Jefferson, 2013). The important variable is how communities managed their inevitable change, not the fact that the change happened.

What Is in a Name

The term *community* is used throughout this book to limit the use of stratifying terms such as *urban, rural, suburban, region,* or just *city*. Those are real and tangible classifications, but rarely does one hear, "I am working to make my suburb or region better." People live in communities. They may be high-rise, low-rise, dangerous, safe, attractive, littered, or spread out, but people still live there and identify with them. Most business locators are less interested in the exact location of their new facility (city or county limits) and more in the overall business climate, quality of life, access to transportation routes, a qualified workforce, and a range of business supports. This is a regional conversation, not just a municipal one. Boundaries, from city limit signs to fire districts to backyard fences, don't tell the whole story. As the demands and opportunities for worldwide economic interactions have become more cemented into our psyche and way of working, traditional boundaries are less important. What hasn't changed, however, is the desire to have the best of both worlds in business location and expansion. While a corporation's decision to locate on one side of the county line or the other may depend on the availability of land, financial concessions, or access to a transportation route, the ultimate decision on where to locate takes into account what the city or region offers.

Community is a term that is used specifically on the one hand and casually on the other. Community evolves around three nexuses: the community of relationships, the community of interests, and the community of place. When the famed Frenchman Alexis de Tocqueville visited America in the nineteenth century, he was impressed by the associational life of Americans: their connections to activities and organizations, their propensity to talk together on issues of mutual concern, and their common concerns about place. The connections and interrelationships of community allow for a stronger and more vibrant civic life. Our lives and fortunes are entangled in ways that de Tocqueville never could have imagined. We have online communities, recreational communities, religious and cultural communities, and geographical communities. People connect themselves in multiple ways, but around these three nexuses: relationships, interests, and place. It is important to understand and build on our varying definitions of community, the new ways of communicating, and the multitude of relationships needed to strengthen our shared social capital in these times of enormous challenge.

So what are communities? They are places where individuals live, connect, work, and are responsible to one another. Sometimes they are called cities, such as Denver; sometimes they are called regions, such as western North Carolina; sometimes they are called cultures, such as Hmong; and sometimes they are just called home, such as Almena, Wisconsin. The most important question is really not what they are but why they are so important. Sampson writes that "communities are an important arena for realizing common values and maintaining effective social controls. As such, they provide an important public good, or what many have termed 'social,' that bear on patterns of social organization and human well-being" (1999, p. 242).

Despite the whirl of bits and bytes, and the eye-blinking speed of the Internet, people and businesses want to live and work in real communities. Writing in the *Harvard Business Review* (1995), Michael Porter makes a compelling case for having one eye focused on the world and one eye focused at home. In theory, he argues, global markets, advanced technology, and high-speed transportation should reduce the role that location plays in business competition. But the opposite is true: a sustainable and competitive economic advantage is rooted in tapping the unique benefits of location. Improving our communities is a critical factor in creating a competitive advantage domestically and globally (p. 58).

When firms and people can locate anywhere and still take advantage of the new economy, place matters more than ever. Planners and community developers often are at a loss to know where to begin. Research done by O'Mara (2005), Segedy (1997), and Klaassen (1993) shows that quality of life is key to economic prosperity as more and more location decisions are made on the ability to attract highly qualified workers. Citizens and leaders with vision have made progress in repositioning cities for different futures and possibilities.

An important development in our more expansive definition of community is the emergence of regions as economic, cultural, and social drivers. We now define regions geographically, culturally, and economically according to specific purposes—where they are and what they sell, grow, make, or do. For example, we speak of the portions of the thirteen states that run along the spine of the Appalachian Mountains as a region. The cities, towns, and villages have strong local identities, but they also have an affinity for and appreciation of the culture of music, food, and mountains that they share. The Fox Cities region of Northeastern Wisconsin includes the cities, towns, and villages along the Fox River as it flows from Lake Winnebago northward into Green Bay. Together they form the core of the third largest metropolitan area of Wisconsin, with a population of almost four hundred thousand. The Fox Cities communities include the cities of Appleton, Kaukauna, Menasha, Neenah, and Oshkosh; the villages of Combined Locks, Hortonville, Kimberly, Little Chute, and Sherwood; and the towns of Kaukauna, Menasha, Neenah, Buchanan, Clayton, Freedom, Grand Chute, Greenville, and Harrison. One of the nation's long-time leading centers of papermaking and printing, the area is diversifying its manufacturing footprint by building a strong foundation of skills and work ethic. Finally, the craft community of western North Carolina has joined together to brand themselves as the "invisible factory" for the arts, design, and craft products they produce.

Recasting what we think of as regions and how local communities can work together for regional purposes is an important component of being globally competitive. In an October 1, 2010, interview with the Federal Reserve Bank of St. Louis, Margery Austin Turner, vice president of the Urban Institute, argues that the answers to our tough community problems require a place, people, and regional lens. Called a place-conscious approach to poverty reduction and job creation, this approach improves where people live and connects them to opportunities and training in the larger region. This kind of strategy steers the conversation about poverty and workforce development away from the urban core and creates a more holistic and comprehensive analysis of the human capital of a region. Thinking about a regional workforce and the power it can bring to an economic development strategy has all positives and almost no negatives. Communities win when they are able to pool their resources with other communities to create a more competitive business environment. Individuals win when they are able to have more job opportunities.

Identifying common interests within and between communities of place is the name of the game. We cannot separate ourselves from one another no matter how hard we try. The suburbs have a stake in the central city; cities have a stake in the suburbs; and rural areas are affected by metropolitan areas and regions. Places that can establish strong identities for themselves while developing relationships with their neighbors hold the greatest promise for economic, social, and civic success.

The Love-Hate Relationship with Cities

A proverbial clash has always existed between American values and "way of life" as they relate to the early American cities as well as today. Historically many people were afraid of cities and their people and environment. Thomas Jefferson referred to them as a "pestilence." These strong feelings—justified or not—have contributed to both the boom and the bust of urban places. People are quite attracted to the glitter and access of cities, but prefer to locate themselves and their families far enough away to avoid the perceived negative aspects such as crime, traffic, and density. In other words, people want to take advantage of the amenities of large urban areas and enjoy more pastoral living elsewhere. They want it all.

Opinion polls show that Americans say that they would prefer to live in a small town; according to a report done by the Pew Research Center (2009), which found that Americans were split in their preference of small town versus big city living, almost one-third preferred a small town versus 23 percent who preferred a city. People value a high quality of life, complete with such things as access to medical care, culture and the arts, recreational opportunities, accessible and affordable housing, business opportunities to make a decent living, and an environment to connect with other people. To put an even finer point on their preferences from the Pew poll, seven of the top ten most popular larger cities were in the West. The Gallup organization conducted a poll in 2012 of almost half a million Americans to determine where they would want to live in 2032, which gave an even clearer picture of their expectations. The verdict: places that have "tackled unemployment, financial concerns, healthcare costs, obesity, and educational challenges" will be the places, says the Gallup Poll, where residents are "healthy, optimistic, have good jobs that they love, and are enthusiastic about where they live." The study found that the future livability of any community will be based on, among other things, its commitment to an entrepreneurial spirit, an informed and active citizenry, and a sense of shared commonwealth. Those places will most likely be in the West North Central region of the country and will include Minnesota, Iowa, Missouri, North Dakota, South Dakota, Nebraska, and Kansas (Witters, 2012).

Smaller cities and towns have much to gain from these preferences. These areas are no longer isolated from the mainstream economic world, which is often associated with big urban centers. They have capitalized on the technology revolution and thrust themselves into the forefront of international business. Distance from the national business epicenters, once considered the death knell of business enterprise, is virtually erased by such now-commonplace aids as Internet sales and real-time communication vehicles such as Skype, Google Hangouts, FaceTime, and a whole range of tools that make distance much less of a consideration.

The last two decades have also seen a sharpening and broadening of our understanding of community. We now think in local as well as regional contexts. As borders touch and issues run past the city limits signs, we must recalibrate our conception of a city or community and its impact. For the purposes of this book and the case illustrations, five organizing units are used: regions, urban areas, "metropolitowns," smaller cities and towns, and rural areas. These categories represent the diversity of where Americans want to live and work.

- *Regions* are defined and undefined geographic, cultural, and commercial areas that house people, places, and business and cultural concentrations that have definable characteristics but not fixed boundaries. The region is evolving as an important unit of organization for cultural, recreational, and economic purposes.

- *Urban areas* run the gamut from New York City and Los Angeles on the one end to Riverside, California, and St. Louis, Missouri, on the other. This category includes those central cities that have the largest populations, with New York City at the top with over eight million people and Riverside, California, at the end of the list with 303,871 (U.S. Bureau of the Census, 2010).

- *Metropolitowns* are places with populations of 50,000 to 250,000. They offer the culture, amenities, and resources of large metropolitan areas while preserving a quality of life often associated with small-town living (Morse, 2004).

- *Small cities and towns* have populations between 10,000 and 49,000. These are often county seats, homes to universities, state capitals, or just places where people live, work, and want their children to stay (U.S. Bureau of the Census, 2010).

- *Rural areas* are communities under 10,000 and can range down to a population of one single person (U.S. Bureau of the Census, 2010).

Size, however, is no guarantee of more interaction among people on issues of common concern; some of the most divided communities are the smaller ones. While cities, towns, and rural areas have unique circumstances because of size, there is less validation today for separating the analysis of their issues than half a century ago. Smaller cities, "metropolitowns," and even rural areas have new issues to address because of changing demographics, access to transportation, and availability of technology. Communities of all sizes no longer are isolated from centers of commerce. They are aggressive economic developers, competing for the attention of national and international firms, developing sophisticated high-technology parks, repositioning their economies, revitalizing their central business districts, and finding ways to make their communities better.

Trends of Growth and Decline of Communities

Historically, as now, both the growth and decline of communities have been caused by a broad spectrum of factors and circumstances. In the nineteenth century, westward movement brought population growth west of the Mississippi. Mining and large parcels of inexpensive farm and ranch land drew people out of the crowded Northeast. A city such as Denver, though land- and mountain-locked, grew rapidly because it was the urban hub for the vast hinterland of ranchers and farmers. The development of cities and towns has challenged the ability to develop a one-size-fits-all national policy to address the varying needs and opportunities.

For most of the last century, America has had conflicting views of how and where to focus attention in cities and towns. Since the thirties, thousands of community development improvement programs have been aimed at stemming the tide of negative change. While there have been some successes; there have been far too few. Neighborhood and rural revitalization efforts have been marked by the invention of new community institutions, by strategic investments in new markets and job training, and by singular interventions to interrelated problem.

It was clear as early as the 1930s, and as late as the 1950s, that America's cities and its rural areas were changing and that the manufacturing and labor-intensive industries that fueled the Industrial Revolution were in decline. Coupled with this economic restructuring was the overlay of racial segregation and immigration that defined patterns of settlement, home ownership, and access to high-quality schools and services. The combination proved deadly for the people who lived in these areas. Historians have analyzed this progression for decades, but for illustration, three policies had a significant impact on every community in America:

• *Federal Housing Administration (FHA):* Enacted in 1934, the FHA changed the mortgage structure to what is in place today. Before the FHA, home buying was precarious at best. After the Great Depression of 1929, home ownership suffered from too few people in financial positions to buy homes, erratic mortgage terms, and a number of homes lost through foreclosure. In order to spur home ownership and secure existing homes, the National Housing Act of 1934 that created the FHA was intended to develop a system to regulate mortgages and initiate a mortgage insurance plan that would provide protection from default for qualified lenders. Amid this important grand scheme for the FHA was a supposed "safeguard," whose consequences changed central cities forever. The process of "redlining" was a component of the housing act that literally color coded neighborhoods in 239 American cities according to standards of occupation, income, and ethnicity to determine residential security and supposedly criteria for ensuring objectivity in awarding mortgage insurance. The color codes referred to: green for new growth areas, blue for still-desirable neighborhoods expected to remain stable, and red for those neighborhoods that were older and where growth and demand were considered past. These "red" neighborhoods housed the majority of African American and minority homeowners and residents. The result of the color-coded system of mortgage insurance made it nearly impossible to sell or buy in inner-city neighborhoods. This, coupled with discrimination in housing, limited the ability of African Americans and other minorities to enter or advance in the housing market. The ensuing disinvestment in central city communities has compounded the myriad of challenges. For individuals, housing provides the most direct pathway to wealth accumulation. While FHA policies have changed and federal law prevents housing discrimination, for many communities the lack of home ownership and the barriers to ownership that early FHA mortgage insurance policies established changed their ability to attract new homeowners—a devastating combination still being felt today.

- *Moving out of the city:* For almost twenty years, through the Interstate Highway Act of 1956, the federal government financed a major public works project to build over 41,000 miles of highway. While the project made the movement of people and goods quicker and more efficient, the highway system left central cities and small towns in its dust. Employment in central cities no longer required that workers live in the same vicinity as their jobs. Cars and the highways made it possible to live in one place and work in another. According to Armbruster (2005), the highway project completely reorganized metropolitan and rural areas in the United States. The central city core experienced the perfect storm for a downward spiral as home building exploded in the burgeoning suburbs, large employers left the city, and middle-class families literally drove away. What we know as urban sprawl began to grow tentacles in unimaginable ways. The major commercial transportation routes, roads famous for their allure such as Route 66 and Highway 1, were no longer the main connecting mediums for most travelers. Once the "bedroom" for recreational travelers, these routes were left without a heavy flow of traffic, but also without the consumers who filled their motels, ate in their locally owned restaurants, and capped off their tanks in strategically placed gasoline stations. While the interstate system cannot be blamed exclusively for the decline of urban core areas and rural byways, it did alter forever the patterns of interaction and levels of investment.

• *Urban renewal:* The Housing Act of 1949 established a process to revitalize central cities and their economies. More than $50 billion in federal funds went to more than two thousand projects intended to eliminate blight in distressed neighborhoods and repurpose the land for economic development. Referred to as "urban renewal," the larger public goal of the act was to thwart the seemingly viral nature of depressed areas and replace them with private development. The planning tool of *eminent domain* was used to acquire whole neighborhoods that stood in the way of major development opportunities. Homes and businesses made way for highways, factories, office buildings, and shopping areas. The justification was that a more prosperous "whole" could contribute to the well-being of the entire community. There is some diversity of opinion about the act and its impact; however, generally speaking, scholars and citizens alike think it was a bad idea overall. The nation and its communities still are feeling the effects of the neighborhood, community, and commercial displacement caused by urban renewal. Divisions caused by this huge public works program, the cyclical investments that followed by private developers, and the disruption to ethnic and racial communities have never been repaired.

These three policies, fueled by globalization, a deconstruction of the traditional manufacturing, agricultural, and extraction economies, a disinvestment in cities, and overt and covert racial discrimination at the policy level, cemented the fate of many urban and rural dwellers and their communities. Places that had once housed immigrants, low-skilled workers, and lower-income working-class families were seen as places to avoid. In many instances, "the projects" was a code for crime and underinvestment. But within those communities were people, institutions, associations, and relationships that could not be defined by the statistics or stereotypes. The fate of neighborhoods following

World War Two resulted from a confluence of external and internal circumstances. The declining numbers of working-class residents had to do with the erosion of the manufacturing and industrial sectors and the jobs they afforded in the central cities, the influx of poorer immigrants, and the loss of revenue that followed (Teaford, 1990, p. 4). A range of actions from suburbanization to urban renewal to a changing economy had major impacts on the positive development of cities and their economic and social foundations.

In the early 1970s another phenomenon occurred: the Sunbelt was identified. Atlanta was in a prime position when the notion of the "Sunbelt" first began to get notice and investment. It became a "world-class city," at its own naming, and began to act like one. As one Georgia trade official commented, "The Sunbelt is not sunshine. It's an attitude . . . conducive to business. The North has lost that attitude." All this boosterism notwithstanding, there has been a resurgence of fortunes of cities from the Deep South to the Southwest to the far West (even Oklahoma added a rising-sun logo to its license plates) (Larsen, 1990, pp. 148–150). This trend is continuing today through automobile manufacturing. Although parts of the Sunbelt are hotbeds of technology, perhaps the most interesting trend is the new auto trail that is being created in this geographic area from South Carolina to Texas.

The Effects of Globalization on Communities

Unquestionably the expansion of a global world—the integration of economic, financial, social, and governing systems—has had the greatest impact on American communities since the Industrial Revolution. Even once we understand what globalization is and how it has come to be, it is still difficult to comprehend the magnitude of its effects on our lives and livelihoods. Primarily, globalization has had four key impacts that affect communities in their efforts to be successful:

1. Transitioning away from manufacturing in the United States
2. Blurring of traditional physical, political, cultural, and economic boundaries

3. Integration that results in the "new economy" (enabled by the blurring of traditional boundaries)

4. Emergence of the local city, community, or region as a critical economic factor (compared to the nation-state)

Transitioning away from manufacturing in the United States. Over the last three decades, the United States has lost five million manufacturing jobs (Deitz and Orr, 2006).

This is mostly due to low wages, cheap operating costs, low restrictions available in Asian and South American countries, and the ease of international trade. The effects have been devastating in some parts of the United States, such as the Rust Belt urban areas of Detroit and Cleveland, whose economies were once centered on manufacturing, and the Southeastern towns with a concentration of textile mills.

Three economists (Auter, Dorn, and Hanson, 2012) studied the effects on U.S. manufacturing of the competition from China. The conclusions were a little mind-boggling. During a sixteen-year period (1991–2007), imports from China grew tenfold. The study found that roughly a million American workers lost their jobs as the result of lower-wage competition from China. While these numbers alone are devastating enough, the authors also documented the twofold "spillover" effect on the communities most hard hit: the businesses no longer bought the local goods and services in the community, and the recently unemployed workers had less disposable income to spend locally and had to rely more on social services.

The shoe manufacturing industry in America is a fitting example of a sector that is rapidly losing ground to global competition. At one time New England dominated the shoe industry in America. Small shops became larger factories, and shoe manufacturing became a staple of the New England economy from Maine to New York. Lynn, Massachusetts, where the shoe lasting machine was invented, called itself the "shoe capital of the world." Today only one company, Alden Shoes, founded in 1884, is still in business in the Northeast. These days most shoes worn by Americans are made in China.

Traditional boundaries blurred. The second impact of globalization is that traditional physical, political, cultural, and economic boundaries are blurred. Part of this arises from a new ability to be multiple places at once. Certainly communication advances have been critical to this. Now we can talk, text, or e-mail someone anywhere in the world for little or no cost. With the introduction of Skype and the concept of video calling, we can even see our partners as we talk. We no longer need to be in our offices to work nor do we need to ever walk into a local bank. We can print our airline tickets at home or load them onto our smartphones. This ease and speed in communication, technology, and travel has spurred a movement toward a more integrated and interdependent world economy.

Integration and the new economy. This blurring of boundaries necessarily leads to greater integration and interdependence among countries, markets, and even cultures. Thomas Friedman (2005) differentiates the present globalization period from the Cold War organization of the world in the mid-twentieth century in this way: we have gone from a system built around division and walls to a system increasingly built around integration and webs. The "new" economy, according to Atkinson and Correa (2007), refers to the period over the last fifteen years in which the structure, functioning, and rules of the economy have been transformed. The New Economy is a global, entrepreneurial, knowledge-based economy in which the keys to success lie in the extent to which knowledge, technology, and innovation are imbedded in products and services" (as cited in Blakely and Leigh, 2010, p. 2).

We see the signs of this everywhere. Richard Florida's (2002) research on "creative communities" put everyone on notice that the work and the workforce were changing. His creative class is defined as "thought leadership," such as artists, writers and editors, analysts, and researchers—people who design a product that can be widely made, sold, and used or an idea or strategy that has broad use. There are also "creative professionals" in his definition—people who manage large amounts of data and work in high-tech or financial services and the legal and health care professions. In 2006 knowledge workers or management comprised more than one-third of all jobs in the United States, while manufacturing jobs accounted for only about 11 percent. Compare that with 1979, when manufacturing jobs accounted for 20 percent.

Emergence of the local community as a critical economic factor. In this new world of blurred boundaries, interconnected economies, and an entrepreneurial, knowledge-based economy, the local community has emerged as a critical economic factor. Globalization affects communities in different ways from how it affects either states or the nation as a whole.

Localities, for the most part, do not control trade policies, tariff restrictions, balance of payments, exchange rates, or intellectual property infringements. Those are left primarily to parties at the national level. However, localities do control who they are and what they do. These are defined most often by two main characteristics: their economy and their quality of life—codependent determinants of a successful community or region.

When firms and people can locate anywhere and still take advantage of the new economy, place matters more than ever. Research done by O'Mara (2005), Segedy (1997), and Morse (2012) shows that quality of life is key to economic prosperity. Likewise a study done by Klaassen (1993) on the Alpine Region of Western Europe showed that employees seek firms in desirable places, and thus more and more corporate location decisions are made on the ability to attract highly qualified workers.

Take Bend, Oregon, for example. A small city in central Oregon, it cut its economic teeth on the timber industry. But things have changed in Bend. Entrepreneurs and business owners were attracted to the small city for its high quality of life—beautiful natural amenities, good schools, world-class healthcare, high-speed Internet, low commute times, and affordable, high-quality housing. In addition, Silicon Valley and Seattle are easily accessible—one hour by plane. The area has continued to spur growth because it is seen as a place that values creativity, innovation, and entrepreneurship. Advances in communication—such as videoconferencing—enable a small place like Bend to compete with larger cities, for example San Francisco, in these arenas. In this way, community and place emerge as critical economic factors. According to Michael Porter (1995), cities and regions are the critical building blocks to competitive advantage:

> Internationally successful industries and industry clusters
> frequently concentrate in a city or region, and the bases for the
> advantage are often intensely local . . . While the national
> government has a role in upgrading industry, the role of state and
> local governments is potentially as great or greater . . . The

> process of creating skills and the important influences on the rate
> of improvement and innovation are intensely local. (pp. 158, 662)

One of the interesting consequences of globalization is that it is no longer necessary to live where you work. Work has changed. Not only do millions of people "telecommute" from their home offices, but many more live on one continent and work on another. To borrow a common catchphrase, we are becoming increasingly more *glocal* (Friedman, 2005, p. 324).

The Mailboxes on Main Street

A growing phenomenon in all communities is increasing diversity. No longer do the mailboxes on Main Street only have names such as Smith, Jones, and Washington. Now they are interspersed with Gonzales, Pham, and Rhon. Coastal cities, as well as traditionally homogeneous landlocked communities, have had a change in their demographic composition. Today forty million foreign-born immigrants live in the United States.

Shifting demographics are perhaps the most significant of the internal changes affecting communities in all locales and of all sizes. The melting pot has moved to middle America. Ethnic grocery stores, places of worship, and non-English radio and television abound in previously homogeneous communities. You do not have to go to Miami, Florida, to attend church services in Spanish; you can go to Allentown, Pennsylvania, or the Blue Ridge Mountains of western North Carolina. Or if you want to understand more about Southeast Asian culture, you can visit Wausau, Wisconsin, New Orleans, Louisiana, or Orange County, California.

Wausau is an interesting example of demographic change. According to the 1980 U.S. Census, Wausau, Wisconsin, was the most ethnically homogeneous city in the nation, with less than 1 percent of the population nonwhite (Beck, 1994). Over the three decades, Wausau has become home to thousands of Hmong immigrants from the mountain tribes of Laos and other Asian ethnicities. Asian students make up 19 percent of the kindergarten through twelfth-grade enrollment in Wausau's school system, and Asians make up 11 percent of the total population of 39,106 (U.S. Bureau of the Census, 2010). A resettlement area for the Lutheran Church, Wausau became home to hundreds of Hmong families fleeing the oppressive government in Laos. Hundreds of communities of all sizes are experiencing significant changes in their populations.

These changes engender different responses. A dichotomy in perception exists about the impact of immigration on communities, as the national debate reflects. Assimilating new people into communities can present challenges and opportunities. Some longtime residents are concerned that the newly settled groups will overburden schools, services, and employment. In areas that are depressed economically, contenders for the few jobs available are resentful when more job seekers enter the pool. However, in a recent article in the *New York Times*, MacDonald and Sampson gave a different view. A recent study done for the *Annals of the American Academy of Political and Social Science* found that although immigrants were poorer and faced hardship, no evidence suggested that they had changed the social and civic fabric of urban, suburban, or rural communities, where they have settled. On the contrary, in many cases they have been instrumental in revitalizing older neighborhoods, helping small towns revive, and perhaps even improving the crime rate. While scholars cannot say with certainty that immigrants were the sole reason for these positive changes, they can say that there was no evidence that immigrants had a negative impact (MacDonald and Sampson, 2012). This seems to square with another part of the equation: the role of immigrants in start-up firms and established companies. According to the Partnership for a New American Economy, roughly 40 percent of Fortune 500 firms were founded by immigrants or their children. But what about Wisconsin—once the most homogeneous state in the United States—what is the impact of the growth of the immigrant population on local job opportunities? " . . . There is no evidence that immigration has a negative impact on native employment," read a 2012 workforce report to Gov. Scott Walker, authored by former Bucyrus-Erie chief executive officer Tim Sullivan. "There is evidence that immigration encourages U.S. natives to upgrade their skills through additional education or training. This would encourage native-born workers to shift into the middle class" (Sullivan, 2012). Sullivan noted that even if Wisconsin retrained every unemployed worker in the state and matched all of them with jobs, it still would fall short of filling the projected 925,000 jobs to be replaced or created by 2018. That's because the state's native-born, working-age population has peaked and will decline over time.

The most successful assimilation experiences occur when services, opportunities for mutual learning and benefit, and a welcome mat work together. Places that make a conscious effort to create opportunities for foreign-born newcomers to engage in their community's life, with language programs, health care translators, job counseling, and places to meet on issues and concerns, seem to do better.

A diverse demographic mosaic can be learned from and embraced. John Gardner's challenge for the demographic diversity of our communities has never been more important. He said that we must create "wholeness out of diversity," that is, embrace our differences as well as our commonality (Gardner, 1990, p. 116). The nation is evolving demographically. With this change comes new challenges and opportunities to make decisions and implement strategies that create communities that welcome, support, and sustain newcomers.

Finding Community Solutions from Within

Over the last several decades, many well-intentioned "solutions" have been applied to communities of all sizes. Whole blocks and neighborhoods have been demolished; whole blocks and neighborhoods have been built; waterfronts have been repaired; downtown cobblestones have been removed; small-business investments have been made; large business incentives have been given. You name it. Some of the many efforts have worked, but by and large the one-size-fits-all solutions have fallen short.

The methods for improving communities that have had the most success are those where nonprofits, business, local government, and citizens have made a commitment and an investment to make their particular situation better. Research has shown that when residents of low-income housing projects get invested, things get better. Evidence further suggests that what distinguishes safe neighborhoods from unsafe ones is not the ratio of police to residents or the frequency of probation offenses, but rather the social fabric of the neighborhood and the condition of the families

(Annie E. Casey Foundation, 1999). When business takes an interest in the schools or when local government incorporates citizens into the decision-making process, things usually get better. Community success is not only possible, it is happening when communities come together.

Ultimately, community success must be measured block by block, neighborhood by neighborhood, and city by city. Despite the glimmers of hope that shine through, just as many community failures take place. The question, of course, is: "Why some places and not others? Why some neighborhoods and not others?" Peirce and Guskind (1993) contend that relationship and civic engagement provide keys to the kind of success every community seeks: "Positive urban breakthroughs rest not so much on electing brilliant people to office—though it is surely handy to have them there—as on the birth of a civic culture of cooperation and a belief in the future, with individuals willing to take up the torch to make that better future a reality . . . " (p. 3). Success, then, is not driven by one political party, a revitalized downtown, or even a new high school; it is about new ways of doing business, different ways of thinking about place and people. As Peirce and Guskind say, "The challenges in American society are far more complex than simply putting roofs over people's heads. They have to do with community" (p. 4). Building the capacity of people to frame and then to solve their own problems is the critical vehicle for civic change and must be the overriding factor as we seek to build and rebuild communities.

These ideas of community, citizen empowerment, and grassroots solutions square with the experiences of communities throughout the United States. Jane Jacobs (1961) was right that billions of dollars will not fix cities, but what will is their own capacity for change and the way they go about their collective work. How people in a community see themselves and one another has everything to do with their well-being and that of their community. If they believe that change can happen, it usually does.

The normal cyclical progression of economies, leaders, and the influence of outside factors affects every community at one time or another. Those that manage these inevitable changes are places that have developed a sense of the future that includes and is shared by the larger community.

New Ways of Working

Stable community-based organizations or development corporations are needed to help define the future and implement strategies for solutions. Diverse coalitions must be established that involve the stakeholders in and out of the affected area (or problem). This includes the need to develop leadership at all levels and to encourage the empowerment of people to affect their own lives. Finally, communities seeking alliances and partnerships to revitalize communities must address persistent concerns about how to deal with race and ethnicity in an increasingly pluralistic society. What are those organizations? Most communities have nonprofit organizations and governmental agencies that work on behalf of the community. However, new research in community development calls for what Brugmann (2009) calls the three faculties of strategic cities: 1) the strategic alliance, 2) local practices of urbanism, and 3) strategic institutions. Brugmann says that you must have a stable, highly committed group of public-private-nonprofit local interests working together toward common goals. These are supported by and illustrated with planning, design, and technical solutions that achieve these goals. And finally, a dedicated strategic institution, "think tank," or research and development arm that diffuses new ideas and strategies is necessary to make change and invention more probable.

The focus for the future must be on how communities can work and work better. Even though history has shown us lessons, directions, and examples of positive change, places have been so bombarded by problems and challenges that there is little time, money, or sometimes even interest to take the long view. Communities and their elected officials have been pressured to do something and do it now. Expediency is one route to take, but community development history is fraught with the results of too much, too fast, too little, or too slow. The Three Bears had the winning combination: just right and a commitment to fundamentals is what we need in the new community model.

Community Fundamentals

Focusing on fundamentals and learning those is where most communities should begin the process of change. We have a whole litany of processes that are embedded within what we refer to as "fundamentals." Think for a minute about accounting, financial investing, or basic arithmetic. Certain things must be done to achieve the next level of success. It is harder to go further if you don't have the basics down pat. In accounting it is the general rules; in investing it is buy low, sell high; and in arithmetic it is addition, subtraction, multiplication, and division. Likewise in sports, certain things are referred to as "essential" if you win the game. In basketball it is free throws; in football it is special teams; in golf it is putting; and in all sports, it is conditioning. Both process and content fundamentals are in community work, too. What are they?

Whether it is a new program, established program, or a response to a crisis or opportunity, communities need to identify and do three key things: 1) know the constituency of stakeholders and the assets they can bring, 2) mobilize diverse stakeholders for discussion and action, and 3) sustain the effort. All three of these things are achievable in any economic climate, under almost any circumstances, and are absolutely fundamental to building a stronger civic and economic infrastructure. The complaints about community enterprises—public, private, or not-for-profit—are that they rely too much on the same voices, the same strategies, and the same plans for sustainability.

Know the stakeholders. Community leaders tend to include people who are known quantities and whose response is predictable as new initiatives are planned and implemented. It is human nature to do this and feels safer and more efficient, the argument being that when groups get too big, it is hard to make a decision. However, this rationale is countered in James Surowiecki's powerful book, *The Wisdom of Crowds*, where he argues for the benefits of collective wisdom in all facets of our lives. Having a multitude of perspectives and voices in a conversation is critical to the outcome. "Ultimately, diversity contributes not just by adding different perspectives to the group but also by making it easier for individuals to say what they really think" (Surowiecki, 2004, p. 39). It is hard to achieve this diversity when who is invited into a community conversation is limited to an inner circle or the same group that came together the last time. A colleague once made an observation of such a situation and asked a simple but powerful question that frames this challenge, "Whom do we need here to help us solve this problem (or realize this opportunity)?"

Get people together and then go in the right direction. Fear and opportunity often evoke the same response: paralysis of action. We hear phrases such as "it is overwhelming," "this is a lot for one group to tackle," or "nothing can get done here if this person or group is not behind it." Naysayers almost always exist, but for every negative voice there is a person or group of persons who thrives on a challenge, sees a way forward through the clouds of dust, and can clarify and organize the small tasks that can reach a much larger goal. Author Jim Collins writes in *Good to Great* (2001) about the organizational "doom loop" that occurs when companies fail to act on what needs to be done to be successful. The failed companies, he observed, did sustain momentum but kept thrashing about looking for the silver bullet. On the community side of the equation, we know that some initiatives don't work and others cannot be sustained over time if funding, support, and strategy are not in place. If the fundamentals are not in place, the vision not clear, the stakeholders not engaged, or the strategy for implementation and sustainability flawed or left to chance, the effort is doomed from the beginning. The warning signs are generally very clear. What Collins tells us from business is that you have to have the right people in place before you can set your vision. His assessment is that if you don't have the right people on board, then the least little bump in the road can derail the group. His famous line, "get the right people on the bus, the wrong people off the bus, and then we'll figure out how to go somewhere great" rings true for community work as well (p. 41). Communities need people committed to a larger vision who have the heart, the patience, and the will to see it through.

Keep the right things going. When Lisbeth Schorr wrote her book *Common Purpose* in 1997, she addressed a very specific question: How can we institutionalize and expand the successful social and educational initiatives around the country to affect millions instead of hundreds or thousands of people? She described three problems from the 1990s that are still with us: collapse of confidence in political institutions and government, citizens' belief that nothing works on a large scale, and rejection of any programs that cost money less out of mean-spiritedness and more out of a feeling of impotence to act on the big issues of the day (pp. xvi–xvii). This description fits two decades later. Too many people don't believe we can tackle the systemic issues facing us and win. The impression is that these problems are too big, too expensive, and just too hard. But we can win if the fundamentals are in place and working.

While a strategy must be crafted to fit the circumstances of an individual place, the world of research and best practice can inform the process and prevent some stumbles. Every community initiative needs a transparent, nonpunitive process of learning and assessing progress that allows for community work to recalibrate. This feedback loop allows the immediate working group, volunteers, funders, and a range of stakeholders to check in on both the process and each other to ensure that work is moving forward. This is what helps small initiatives grow in size and impact.

The *Smart Communities* framework and supporting case vignettes suggest a strategy for applying fundamentals in community work. The seven points are not "either/or" but rather a clear, comprehensive direction of what must be in place for the real breakthroughs in a community to occur. The pieces fit together in a pattern. Communities are rich mosaics of size, people, institutions, traditions, and even problems. For our purposes, the new pieces are the proven strategies for success that are found in the following seven leverage points. They broaden and enrich the notion of community for everyone. Change strategies really work only when they include all people in creating a new picture. It is not enough, however, to eliminate the negatives; we must also cultivate and invest in the value-added positives. Successful community efforts have found the right combination of community investments and amenities that foster, cultivate, and encourage a different kind of place for the community and economic activity. As people in communities look for answers, the ideas and solutions may come from places unlike their own.

CHAPTER TWO

Investing Right the First Time

In 1883 the Minneapolis Board of Trade established an independent park commission to preserve and protect parkland and green space. The board believed that securing land then for what they called "the finest and most beautiful system of public parks and Boulevards of any city in America" would add many millions to the future value of real estate in the city. Despite objections by the city council that the commission lacked accountability and oversight, the voters approved the creation of the commission (Speltz, cited in Garvin, 1996, p. 64).

The creation of the park commission; the hiring of two well-known landscape architects, Frederick Law Olmstead and H.W.S. Cleveland; acquiring land before it was needed; and finally, recognizing the future costs of maintaining a first-quality public open space were critical to the park system's long-term success. As a result, the city acquired thousands of acres that were set aside and provided the system with an income stream, an elected administrative structure, and the legal power to ensure that the parks would be maintained (Garvin, 1996, p. 69).

This smart investment has paid off. The sixty-four hundred acres in the system are designed so that there is one acre of parkland for every sixty-six citizens, or every home within six blocks of a park. The property and land values of park-adjacent neighborhoods and downtown property have shown enormous increases. Every nickel spent on the parks and green space yields a twentyfold return (Koerner, 1998). But just as important, the commission has mechanisms to support, preserve, and enhance the original investment. This exemplar of investing right the first time illustrates the importance of the initial decision but just as important the forethought and strategy that ensured that the investment was sustained. This 130-year decision is in every sense of the word a strategic investment that has paid enormous dividends economically, socially, and environmentally.

Albert Einstein once said, "Intellectuals solve problems, geniuses prevent them." While a bit grandiose, actually Mr. Einstein was right: prevention is cheaper and more effective. As a craftsperson said to me, "There is no profit in redo." Yet we "redo" all the time in our community work. We hope beyond hope that our worst fears won't be realized, that what will likely happen . . . won't. We hope, for example, that poorly funded schools will have miraculous results or that people without the proper training can be the workforce of the future or that the environment will clean itself. We have operated on a hope and wish for generations now. We find ourselves in the quandary of experiencing a growing demand for services and resources but meeting that with declining revenues and capacity. We could give up right now or we can begin to do what Mr. Einstein suggests—prevent some problems.

With money tight, demands high, and taxes of all kinds unpopular, some key areas of our economic and quality-of-life strengths are getting short shrift. We call these the "wicked" problems, issues that require a range of investments to solve and have no finite technical solution. In short, these are the tough ones: poverty, environmental decline, and educational attainment, to name just a few. The choices presented: delay investments in these issues and pay later or invest now and reap the benefits indefinitely are the ongoing challenges for communities. The best investment and life advice I ever got was, "to make long-term gains, you must do well when the market is down." In community terms, we cannot count on an uptick all the time or perfect circumstances to address the problems; communities have to act on the opportunities at hand. They must have a strategy for investment that puts them in the best position for success.

I happened to be in Minneapolis on August 2, 2007, when the bridge over the Mississippi River collapsed. As the horror unfolded on television, most people were saying and thinking the same thing: "We have to do something about those bridges." Now almost a decade later, we *still* have unsafe bridges. In the meantime, there has been a major recession, an exploding deficit, continuing military involvement abroad, and increasing demands on local, state, and national budgets, but there are still too many unsafe bridges. A 2013 report by the American Society of Civil Engineers maintained that one out of all nine bridges is deficient, which translates to 210 million trips taken by motorists across an unsafe bridge every day in the 102 largest metropolitan areas. The reality is that the bridges are not going to fix themselves. Reports and warnings are most helpful when they lead to action; communities have to invest in key issues and projects when times are tight and the timing is not perfect.

The same logic can be applied to the nation's most pressing social and economic challenges—they will not fix themselves. If young children are not reading at level at eight years of age, most likely they will not be at twelve unless an intervention occurs. The nation's educational system has been at risk for decades. The outcomes are crystal clear: too few students finishing the minimal rung on the ladder—high school, a workforce lagging behind in some key areas, and a surplus of jobs available with too few qualified applicants. The "fix" could begin in Washington, D.C., or it could begin in communities, where action can be taken and the results seen up close and personal. On a visit to Richmond, Indiana, in 2007, one statistic got people thinking: if children are not reading at grade level in the fourth grade, they might not ever be. Faced with just this problem, Richmond's action strategy is illustrative of what all communities have to do when faced with a problem: make a plan and implement it. Within a few months the community created The Third-Grade Reading Academy to improve the reading skills of about 30 percent of the students finishing third grade who needed some summer help. Using an innovative curriculum, two businesspeople solicited the help of the school system, local organizations, parents, and others to join together to get all fourth-grade students in Richmond reading at grade level. Testing showed that this kind of investment and intervention has made a difference. The National Civic League thought so, too, in recognizing the community with its All-America City Award in 2009 identifying the Academy as a major initiative. However, this kind of local success and national recognition did not lessen the pressures of fundraising for the Academy. Even great programs such as this one are hard to sustain.

No matter the severity of obstacles, the barriers, or the lack of public will, communities must work together to fix the things that need fixing. On the business side, return on investment (ROI) and risk management are discussed with great regularity. Essentially, communities have to go through the same process as they evaluate the return that they both want and need, and as important, the consequences of not investing. There will never be enough money to solve all of our problems—never has been even when heavy federal investment was forthcoming. Rather, the solutions will come from a combination of money, strong public will, stakeholder engagement, and creative collaborations. If all these factors are not in place, progress will be slow if possible at all.

This chapter discusses ways that communities can build an investment strategy that yields returns over the long run. It develops the idea that communities need investment portfolios and strategies, just as individuals do. In order to achieve results on the systemic issues of our day—the things people really care about—communities must think more strategically about how to invest, where to invest, and when to invest. This requires more knowledge about what works, more information about the range of resources that can be applied to the issue, and finally, a clear communication strategy to the whole community. All of this requires that government, organizations, and community members get out of siloes and familiar territory and talk to each other about ways to ensure a common future that works and lasts. This chapter will look at the challenges and rewards of a clear and strategic community investment strategy that calls on and develops all kinds of capital through the lens of Portland, Oregon; Seattle, Washington; and Ann Arbor, Michigan. All three of these cities epitomize one defining principle of successful community work: they set goals and meet them. Sometimes things just happen but, more likely, a group of people makes them happen.

The Wicked Problems

We all know them when we see them. We ride through neighborhoods that seem to decline more every time we go there. We read about increasing demands on food banks and shelters. We see the effects of poverty in high crime numbers, low educational achievement, and lack of prenatal care. We see years of abuse and under-regulation in the warnings at lakes and rivers closed for swimming and fishing. These are not problems that can be fixed with a government grant to one locality. These are the most complex issues we face in society, whose impact goes far beyond this generation. In *Wicked Problems: Problems Worth Solving*, Kolko (2012) defines a wicked problem and its complexity in this way. It is a "social or cultural problem that is difficult to solve for four reasons: 1) incomplete or contradictory knowledge; 2) the high number of stakeholders, people, and opinions involved; 3) the potential of a large financial burden to make progress; and 4) interconnection with other problems."

First named as "wicked" problems by Rittel and Webber (1973), who compared them to the "tame" problems associated with mathematics, chess, and puzzles, these kinds of problems are so complex and interrelated that they cannot be solved by a technical solution; there is no agreement among the "experts" on the solution; and there is conflicting information about the cause, culprit, and impact. While the public is aware of these problems, there is a general feeling that there is little if anything that can be done—they are beyond reach. So, instead of chipping away, we too often just look away. According to Rittel and Webber, "The search for scientific bases for confronting problems of social policy is bound to fail because of the nature of these problems . . . Policy problems cannot be definitively described. Moreover, in a pluralistic society there is nothing like the indisputable public good; there is no objective definition of equity; policies that respond to social problems cannot be meaningfully correct or false; and it makes no sense to talk about 'optimal solutions' to these problems . . . Even worse, there are no solutions in the sense of definitive answers" (1973, p. 155).

Rittel and Webber assign ten characteristics to wicked problems that include their lack of a transferrable definition—the causes and solutions to poverty in one place may be different from other places; it is almost impossible to claim success or evaluate the impact on a problem because of its links to other problems; there is no template for solving these problems, although research and best practice can be a guide; and there is a context and uniqueness to every wicked problem (1973, pp. 155–169). The realization that the issues we have abhorred and railed against may be with us indefinitely is hard to swallow. We cannot stop working on poverty because it affects all of us; we cannot stop improving our water, air, and climate because it affects all of us; and we cannot stop investing in children, no matter the negatives associated with their parents, because their future affects all of us.

In the first edition, this chapter focused on just this kind of wicked issue—high school dropouts. At that time, there was not much discussion at the national or local levels on either the definition or the implications of the problem. In fact, there was no uniform calculation of the dropout number, and many school systems undercounted and underestimated the severity of the problem as a result. But knowledge plus realization changed the national conversation. In 2004 Robert Balfanz and Nettie Legters from Johns Hopkins University coined a term, "dropout factories," to describe high schools where fewer than 50 percent of the students graduate. That label and their corresponding research that certain schools had "weak promoting power," where graduation was not the norm, and that those schools were disproportionately divided by race caught national attention. This research underscored that "The dropout issue is one of a myriad of issues requiring a clear investment strategy, as communities consider asset allocation, program priorities, and economic development. Statistics have shown that the long-term cost of a student dropping out of high school affects individual earnings, prevents the development of needed skills and competencies, and can create a significant financial burden in lost taxes and wages" (Morse, 2004, pp. 22–23).

In the last decade, there have been major initiatives at the national, state, and local levels to begin to address this problem. Building on the strong foundation of the National Dropout Prevention Center and Communities in Schools, a host of organizations are connecting dropout prevention to issues such as workforce development, youth well-being, and community success. The National Governor's Association is working with governors at the state level to address the problem; America's Promise Alliance Grad Nation has enlisted the help of businesses, communities, schools, and a whole range of stakeholders to address the problem; the Learning to Finish campaign launched by Civic Change, Inc., is mobilizing citizens in local communities to get all students ready for ninth grade; and the National Education Association's comprehensive research and multibillion-dollar commitment will invest in prevention over the next decade. Many communities across the country have intensive programs on retention, dropout prevention, and ways for citizens to help. Jacksonville, Florida, is one of those cities that has connected Communities-in-Schools, Learning to Finish, and America's Promise Alliance to build a broad-based constituency to address the problem from all angles. Cedar Rapids, Iowa, has integrated strong prevention programs into their school system. Collaborative groups have formed across the country to tackle this wicked problem that impacts the lives of so many young people and their communities. Change can happen when communities invest the time, money, and will in their solutions.

The dropout crisis is far from solved, but it illustrates that wicked issues can be addressed if creative solutions are crafted, stakeholders have an opportunity to think together, and blame is off the table. Wicked problems will not fix themselves; they need all of the community's expertise and creativity and an investment strategy that pays dividends.

Another issue that captured attention in recent years is the relationship of healthy babies and prenatal care. Vermont, like every other state, had seen the long-term effects suffered by babies whose mothers did not receive prenatal care during pregnancy, such as low birth weight, increased hospital stays for baby and mother, and higher infant mortality rates. Preterm babies are a national challenge, which according to the March of Dimes affects more than half a million babies each year. The Institute of Medicine estimates that this health issue costs the nation $26 billion annually in medical, education, and low-productivity costs. During the 2010–11 legislative session, a request came to the Department of Vermont Health Access for a preliminary analysis of the benefits of having a program for high-risk pregnancies among Medicaid recipients. The results showed that care management and care coordination could prevent certain complications. So armed with convincing information, Vermont took action. The legislature convened a work group, an agreement was reached on a definition of "high risk," and the 2010 Medicaid claims analysis showed fourteen hundred high-risk pregnancies during CY 2010, representing approximately 40 percent of all pregnancies in this cohort group. The estimated cost savings from an intervention was estimated to be almost half a million dollars. The work group then identified existing programs and care providers, established a structure for coordination, and began to think about how to implement the program (Joint Fiscal Committee, September 26, 2011).

The Vermont example illustrates that identifying a program, gathering relevant data, investing in finding solutions, and developing partnerships can solve problems and save money. Investing in solutions is far more cost-effective than paying for remedies.

Kinds of Community Capital

Investment capital comes in different forms, but generally falls into the following eight categories:

- *Human capital* refers to investments in people and their skills. It usually includes formal schooling as well as technical training and workforce development. In the classical economic sense, these investments increase the output of the worker.

- *Physical or built capital* generally is considered to be the built infrastructure of a community and the investments needed to operate it safely and efficiently. In addition to the basic requirements of roads, sewers, and bridges, there are added dimensions such as power plants or energy sources, broadband connections, and water quality treatment facilities.

- *Community capital* includes what we might think of as development capital, such as affordable housing, youth centers, arts and cultural centers, recreational opportunities, and public spaces that bring people together.

- *Financial capital* provides access to affordable dollars and credit markets. This form of capital has been particularly challenged by the 2007–2009 Great Recession and its aftermath as banks and other financial institutions restricted the money available for mortgages, housing starts, and business development.

- *Environmental or natural capital* encompasses an area's natural resources, including water, air, wildlife, and vegetation and the management of those components as well as parks, trails, and green space.

- *Political capital* is the ability to get things done and the access to and credibility with elected and appointed officials.

- *Social capital* is the relationships that exist among community members that make action possible. Putnam (2000) expands the understanding of social capital with the delineations between bridging and bonding capital. *Bridging social capital* occurs within groups of people who work for common purposes: people in the same vocational field, coalitions of people concerned about an issue, or even communities that choose to work together for a common purpose in a region. *Bonding capital* usually is built or enforced within a social or organizational circle. These are the people you choose to be with: personal friends, family, club members, peers, and so on. Bridging capital is more inclusive than its cousin bonding capital. According to Putnam, "bonding social capital constitutes a kind of sociological super glue, whereas bridging social capital provides a sociological WD-40" (pp. 22–24).

- *Integrative capital* is the intersection between the seven types of capital that allows all to prosper.

In their analysis of the interrelation of different forms of capital, Emery and Flora (2006) argue that it is the synergies among the types of capital that build and strengthen the social capital needed to spur new development efforts. Using the Community Capitals Framework for assessment, they argue that holistic community change happens when human, financial, natural, cultural, social, political, and built capitals intersect, impact all capitals, and increase the community's ability to act in concert on an array of issues. Rural communities are accustomed to the downward spiral caused by the decline in agriculture, the out-migration of jobs, and the brain drain. In one Nebraska town, Emery and Flora tested ways that capital integration can help communities "spiral up." Spiraling up results when one or more categories of assets increase the likelihood of increases in other forms of capital (Gutierrez-Montes, 2005). This cumulative causation becomes an almost self-fulfilling prophecy for the community as success begets success (p. 33).

Rarely does one kind of capital—the renovation of one building or the designation of one area—jumpstart the whole economy, but one thing can be a catalyst for more things to come. As Emery and Flora write, the integration of different types of assets is a cascading, synergistic process that takes time, collaboration, and investments. The "tipping point" occurs when a "cluster" of companies, arts venues, restaurants, historical sites, and recreational opportunities reinforce and build on each other. Table 2.1 shows the types of community investments and related activities.

How Decisions Are Made . . . Matters

The process of making community decisions about the priority and importance of investments requires both a normative and descriptive approach—that is, how decisions *should* be made and how they *are* made in real-life situations. This is where the real community learning occurs. Community members need to know that there are ways to make decisions that include multiple voices and perspectives. When this process is short circuited or not done at all, the community suffers. Safford (2009) provides some insights about process and results in his analysis of the decision-making processes in Allentown, Pennsylvania, and Youngstown, Ohio, and the economic, social, and civic networks that supported them. His research showed that good decision making is built on the diversity of voices in the change process and an openness to change itself.

After World War II, a significant decrease in demand for steel in the United States posed a serious threat to cities such as Allentown and Youngstown—the lifeblood of their economies. But how they responded to the situation made all the difference. In Youngstown, the community could not agree on a plan of action to diversify the economy and reposition itself. Longtime community leaders, an insular group comprised of just a few families, disagreed on a change strategy and even the need for one. They were blind to the permanent evolution in the world economy, shifts in the labor force, the movement away from manufacturing, and a declining demand for U.S.-made steel. Few significant

Table 2.1. Examples of Types of Community Investments

Human Capital	Social Capital	Community Capital	Physical Capital
Public education	Athletic leagues	Museums	Roads and highways
Literacy programs	Volunteer centers	Parks	Historic buildings
Pre-K education	Community gardens	Affordable housing	Bicycle lanes
Job training	Block clubs	Cultural centers	Libraries
Alternative education	Farmers' markets	Festivals	Sewer, water, and power systems
Apprentice academies	Dance groups	Youth centers	Broadband infrastructure

Financial Capital	Environmental Capital	Political Capital	Interactive Capital
Community credit unions	Natural resource management	Access to decision makers	Wellness programs
Community reinvestment programs	Sustainable agriculture	Open government	Collaborative planning
Small business loan funds	Water quality programs	Local leadership development	Community indicators
Homebuyer counseling	Natural areas	Neighborhood improvement funds	Public space
Venture capital funds	Biophilic design	Deliberative dialogues	Cross jurisdictional partnerships
Angel investors	Green space and parks	Town meetings	Cultural resources

Note: For an expanded discussion of these forms of community capital investments, see Green and Haines, 2002, pp. 81–100 (human capital); Putnam, 2000, pp. 22–28 (social capital); and McNulty, 1993, pp. 231–249 (civic capital).

proactive measures were taken to protect Youngstown from the inevitable changes that were occurring. The unwillingness of community and corporate leadership to repackage, redesign, or innovate was based on the idea that they were experiencing a few bad years for the steel industry, which would soon resurrect itself. Essentially Safford's network analysis shows too much bonding capital. That is, the business and civic elites were the same people; they only talked to themselves.

Allentown, however, was a community organized with overlapping as well as independent connections between business, government, and nonprofit leaders. This kind of diversification led to a more robust set of ideas to help leverage the old economy to the new. Since the 1950s, Allentown's technological evolution positioned it to react to change in positive ways. The original Western Electric plant built in 1948 has had continual retooling over the years beginning with electronic tubes, then transistors a few years later, then satellite communications, microelectronics, and solid-state technology. A close working relationship between Lehigh University researchers, workers, scientists, unions, and management made these changes not only possible but also feasible.

Safford describes the different approaches by the two communities as the high road and the low road. The high-road community, Allentown, transformed local companies by integrating technology, production, and strong industrial relationships; supporting entrepreneurs; and creating an atmosphere of trust among workers and management. The low-road community, Youngstown, set the bar for whatever jobs it could attract, fostered a negative atmosphere between workers and management, and never really leveraged its local university and new economic opportunities. It is a shrinking city, some would argue, because it couldn't conceive of a bigger world and new opportunities. Still challenged, Allentown was able to grow and adjust with its largest employers and readjust as the corporations unbundled or moved.

Setting Priorities on Community Investments

The reality is that all communities share many of the same challenges. While some are more affected than others, there are no perfect scores in community and economic development efforts. Most places are worried about their educational attainment, the training of their workforce, and the long-term future of people at the bottom of the socioeconomic scale.

Places that took a chance on an investment strategy two or three decades ago are reaping the results of their investment today. Strategic community investments can produce dividends for individuals as well as the community over time. These investments compound—they just keep on giving. Albert Einstein once remarked that compound interest was the greatest discovery ever made! What he meant, of course, is that being strategic about investments allows the investor to reap rewards without doing much. In his example, money makes money on the community side; the better we do, the stronger the rewards.

At first glance, the priority of investments or budget allocations seems obvious. The "low hanging fruit" would have to be such things as education, housing, and infrastructure. While these areas are critical and sometimes are targeted of necessity, it is important to consider the development of a community's portfolio in a more holistic way. Communities set on an investment strategy that fuels the economic engine at the expense of quality of life lose. A balanced approach to community investment considers a range of areas in a community—the needs, opportunities, and amenities needed to build a strong economy and a high quality of life for all community members in order to encourage growth, participation, and business location and expansion. How does a community decide how to invest in one thing over another? Aren't the public schools more important than a new baseball stadium? There is no either-or answer. With limited revenues coming into communities, the decision on how to allocate resources for the greatest return must be driven by the community's strengths, by the areas that will fill out its competitive profile, and by the greatest need. An example of this decision-making process might be the need to increase the number of jobs. The investment strategy could be improving the skills of the workforce to attract new businesses or providing incentives for companies to relocate or offering a venture fund to support young entrepreneurs. Most communities say, "We need all of that and more. Where do we begin?" This is where the portfolio analogy is most helpful. Attention must be paid to a range of investments to get to the larger bottom line. In the same way that an investment goal might mean a certain monthly income at retirement, communities need to have a larger goal and then a cascading set of objectives to achieve that goal. Even if every person in the community had access to job training, but the community had little to offer in the way of quality of life, it might not be fruitful to continue to invest solely in job training; it would be time for a balanced portfolio approach.

More Than Just a Bottom Line

Almost every community has a comprehensive plan, and a fair number have benchmarking projects that provide a frame of reference on certain variables at any given time. For a community to build a thriving future—one sustainable for the next generation—that community or region needs to have a clear understanding of where it stands, where it wants to go, *and* the strategy and priorities that must be set to achieve its goals.

Often these community markers are defined as indicators. According to the Institute for Sustainable Development, " . . . an indicator quantifies and simplifies ideas and concepts and helps us understand complex realities. They are aggregates of raw and processed data to form new indices." While this process is helpful for most communities, unless indicators are generated with considerable civic participation and a link to budgeting, the data and the subsequent indicators can be little more than wish lists with no action plan or strategy to accompany them. The biggest flaws in the indicators process are the lack of recognition of the interrelationship of the data, multiple correlations around issues that interact and affect one another, and the lack of an action strategy.

One of the earliest communities to adopt an indicators approach, a group called Sustainable Seattle, released its first set of indicators in 1998, stating that the objective was a "call to action" that would spur critical thinking, reconsider priorities, and leverage action. At first glance, the group's categories and indicators seem satisfactory and reasonable—for example, voter participation, unemployment, and air quality. However, on closer inspection, they give little instruction, other than what is implied—that is, "reduce carbon footprint"—to guide the "how to" and "how much" questions that would surely follow. In 2006 the board realized that the publishing of indicators was just not enough and called for the community's indicators project to be halted temporarily. In order to be effective, the board said, the indicators needed to be accompanied by strategies that citizens, policymakers, and business leaders could implement to affect the trends suggested by the indicators. The data should drive change, not just inform the community.

What we have learned from the experiences of Seattle and other communities that have strong indicators initiatives is that the indicators need an action agenda to support their implementation. The data collected and the decisions made must have an overarching strategy that leads to a new reality. Maclaren (2004) instructs that community data should present a complete picture. It must:

- Integrate economic, environmental, and social conditions
- Be futuristic and consider the impact and equity on future generations
- Be distributional and consider a wide range of individuals and areas
- Have input from stakeholders
- Be useful in decision making (Harmon, 2008)

In other words, data collection and analyses must be coupled with the impact and implications related to other areas of the community and the budget to support them. Rather than providing an incremental or a program budget, the "smart" budgeting scenario would give community members and policymakers a better idea of how money is being spent, the impact of one issue on another, and the demand on expenditures.

These kinds of parameters set direction for the action steps from the outset and are codified in a term called *The Triple Bottom Line.* It is not enough to look at one set of challenges in isolation; they must be weighed and addressed in relation to other factors over time. Coined by Englishman John Elkington, a British business consultant who founded SustainAbility, the concept was intended to capture a larger scope for investments, first by the corporate world and later by communities. The triple bottom line as Elkington envisioned it was to measure a company's "planet" account, which consists of profit, people, and planet impacts. The point is to add value to a financial investment while incorporating other community values and priorities. These are the kinds of choices that communities face all the time ("Triple Bottom Line," 2009). For example, in 2013 the City of Wilmington, North Carolina, a desirable coastal community that has invested heavily in its quality of life in recent years, was embroiled in a controversy regarding jobs versus the environment. Titan America wanted to build one of the nation's largest cement and strip-mining operations along the Cape Fear River that runs near Wilmington. Critics argued that it would destroy one thousand acres of wetlands and wildlife habitats, add to the air pollution, and withdraw up to sixteen million gallons of water each day from nearby aquifers, possibly lowering the water tables. Supporters, including the company, countered that the impact will be much less and that the wetlands will be mitigated at a larger ratio than those actually impacted. Further, the economic impact would include 160 new, full-time jobs and a fiscal return of $120 to $133 million within five years. The question is whether jobs and capital investment trump environment and quality-of-life concerns. This kind of dilemma calls for a triple bottom line analysis.

The most common kinds of results from investments tend to hover around the jobs created, costs reduced, and dollars leveraged. However, these do not allow for a full vetting. To assist communities through the process, the U.S. Economic Development Administration has created an online tool to help communities assess their investments from multiple perspectives. In a series of questions included in an online form, investors, economic development professionals, and decision makers can weigh the impact of their decisions about projects and begin to consider how to communicate the value of triple bottom line investments. The tool (http://tbltool.org) has three primary benefits: 1) to optimize project impact (design tool), 2) to compare projects or investments (decision tool), and 3) to disseminate information about impact (communication tool) (Hammer, Babcock, and Moosbrugger, 2012).

The immediacy of the world economy, the increasing competition from the town next door or the city in Asia, and the desire to live in a place other than cyberspace requires that we assess, analyze, and act on community diagnostic information in new ways and create a model of action that shows the relationship between issues but also informs, galvanizes, and directs action. Community members, policymakers, and students need the best possible data and the tested practices to craft place-based strategies for change. If the community is to invest wisely for the long term, at the end of the day action must be taken to solve problems. Far too many reports, visioning exercises, community goal-setting, and strategic plans collect dust rather than doers.

Finding a Guide for Investment Success

After the last decade of working with communities on their investment portfolios, a consistent question has been raised: How should the community structure their investments and what should their priorities be? The answer is informed by three things. (1) The community must know where the areas of greatest need and leverage are. This is driven by data, potential impact, the opportunity costs of not investing, and a gauge of the public will to act, assessments must be made. (2) There must be a more holistic view of the investment. It is critical that community members think about how investments interrelate and support the overall goal of a stronger, more prosperous community. This is where the balanced portfolio is important and civic engagement essential. Capital investments done wisely and strategically reinforce each other and create different scenarios. (3) Community decision making must be driven by specific targets and areas of priority. These can vary by community. For example, some communities focus on water availability and accessibility while others worry more about unemployment. To move an action agenda from the general to the particular, residents must be well educated on the issues and the choices before them. For example, accessible, available, and affordable quality water is becoming a global crisis. In the United States and elsewhere in the world, the impact of pollution, climate change, and poor land use choices have wreaked havoc on our rivers and streams. Technologically, we can do some things to improve our national water system, but this is a problem that cannot be "fixed" by a technical solution. It requires a change in behavior and priorities by a broad range of stakeholders. This kind of wicked issue is indicative of the kinds of issues that drive the community agenda, that require civic engagement at all levels and ways to prioritize community, state, and national investments.

Despite their individual differences and characteristics, the strongest communities in the nation are those in which citizens across the economic and social spectrum have access to affordable housing and health care, and high-quality education; where robust arts and entertainment sectors and physical amenities such as parks are present and accessible; and where finding a living-wage job is not only possible but probable. These indicators are the outcomes of a strong economy and a high quality of life. These are relatively easy to measure. Less easy to measure are the intangibles that complete the scenario: social capital, relationship among the sectors, and level of civic engagement. Communities have to decide what is important to them and what they are willing to pay for in terms of money and time. However, it is not always about the place that spends the most. In the research on educational attainment in the nation, there is a clear connection between the amount of investment in education and the eventual outcomes. Two states—Vermont and New Hampshire—invest more generously in education, and their outcomes reflect that investment. But there are some states such as Iowa that get a big bang for their educational buck. A successful investment strategy uses all the resources available to reach the goal.

While there is no perfect numerical formula, there is a body of research and tools that communities can use to guide their thinking and jumpstart the process of change. Certain circumstances require that communities decide what they need to do and then work backward to establish their goals. For example, by using a tool called ANSWERfirst®, developed by Civic Change, Inc., communities can develop a transparent action strategy around a set of priorities related to economic prosperity and quality of life. Figure 2.1 illustrates this process. The exercise allows the participant to set a goal and to generate a range of options to reach the goal. It is an outgrowth of the Thriving Communities model that has correlated twelve quality-of-life and economic prosperity variables in 358 metropolitan statistical areas to

Figure 2.1. ANSWERfirst®

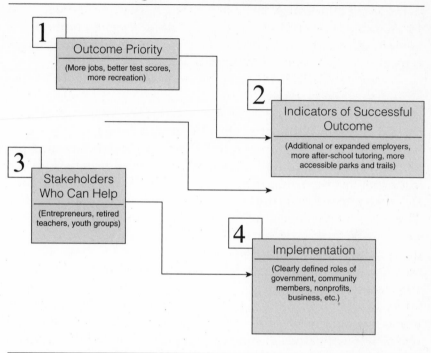

determine where each variable is getting the best results. Ann Arbor is one of the cities included in the Thriving Communities model that performed strongly on all twelve variables and was in the top 5 percent of all places studied. Its investment strategy is yielding returns on all fronts. Communities such as Ann Arbor are instructive in showing how and where key investments are made.

Ann Arbor, Michigan: A City on the Hunt

Home to the University of Michigan and its Wolverines, Ann Arbor is at the top of many "livable cities" lists. Less than twenty-five miles from Detroit, Ann Arbor sits in stark contrast to the issues that have plagued America's original motor city for decades. A city of roughly two hundred thousand people, it boasts a well-educated workforce, a strong infrastructure, easy access to major transportation hubs, a culture of innovation and entrepreneur-ism, the talents of many people, a strong educational system, and an abundance of natural resources. Among the economic devel-opment engines in Ann Arbor is SPARK, a public-private partner-ship cofounded by Governor Rick Snyder and partners at the University of Michigan in 2005 (Ann Arbor SPARK, 2006). This partnership works to advance the area as a desired place for busi-ness expansion and location and to capture the talent graduating from the area schools by identifying and meeting the needs of business at every stage, from established corporations to start-ups. SPARK also provides education and training as well as funding resources for entrepreneurs, business engagement and support, an incubator network, and services for established companies as well as job seekers, rounding out a full range of offerings to ensure that Ann Arbor's business community will survive and thrive for many years to come. Finally, it makes funding available for an internship program to assist early-stage small companies and start-ups that otherwise would be unable to afford interns.

SPARK is only one of a range of investments that Ann Arbor is making to anchor its economy and high quality of life. Pure Michigan asset-based economic development incentives provide funds for business attraction, economic gardening, business accel-eration, and film and digital media; and in January 2012, Michi-gan's new corporate income tax, which is more business friendly and encourages investment, replaced the business tax. Ann Arbor also has a well-established Downtown Development Authority and local business associations that have worked to establish Ann Arbor as a twenty-four-hour city through implementation of such initiatives as alternative transportation programs, energy audits for downtown building and business owners, affordable housing projects, and support for downtown events.

Contributing to the vibrancy of downtown Ann Arbor is an active arts scene, featuring a range of cultural offerings from art exhibits to performances by jazz legends. Downtown Ann Arbor is home to more than thirty independent bookstores and a number of galleries and museums, including the recently reno-vated Ann Arbor Hands-On Museum. Regional and local per-forming arts groups include the Ann Arbor Civic Theater, the Arbor Opera Theater, the Ann Arbor Symphony Orchestra, the Ann

Arbor Ballet Theater, the Ann Arbor Civic Ballet, the Ark, and the Performance Network Theater. The community resources are complemented by a myriad of programs at the University of Michigan.

Ann Arbor's population is highly educated: almost two-thirds of residents have four years of college or more. The city's public schools support a Health Science Technology program and a Rising Scholars program, a partnership between the University of Michigan Center for Educational Outreach and Ann Arbor Public Schools designed to assist underserved but high-achieving students in decreasing the documented achievement gap and preparing them for college. The Ann Arbor Public Schools Education Foundation furthers the good work of the public schools, facilitating private giving and administering Initiatives for Excellence programs designed to enable students, teachers, and the community to thrive through dispersing a variety of grants and scholarships to support the next generation.

Finally, Ann Arbor's well-established Neighborhood Watch Program helps maintain the city's low crime rate, and Ann Arbor has superior access to health care as a result of the University of Michigan's 30 health centers and 120 outpatient clinics. The VA Ann Arbor Healthcare Systems (VAAAHS) also provides high-quality, cost-effective care to Ann Arbor's veterans and conducts a plethora of research initiatives because of a substantial annual research budget of approximately $10.6 million.

Ann Arbor understands what it means to have a balanced community portfolio. The community has joined their funding and support with an action and implementation agenda that is multipurposed and targeted. The results speak for themselves.

Choosing the Right Investment: Creating New Scenarios for Change

It would be nice if there were a community crystal ball to help us decide what to do and when. Unfortunately, we don't have such a tool for Main Street or Wall Street. Ultimately investment decision making rests with process—how we decide what is most important, an alert system—that allows community members to know and understand the implications of an issue, and an evaluation or assessment process based on community learning and not community blame. The level of investment should match the seriousness of the issue. Such foundational issues as early childhood education, public health, and workforce development must be considered as priority areas that could have the greatest overall impact on the community, as Ann Arbor illustrates. But quality-of-life issues matter, too. Access to recreation, numbers of cultural opportunities, and environmental quality are critical components of a long-term competitiveness agenda. A question that citizens, organizations, and governments should be asking and answering in a deliberative way is this: Are we funding stopgap measures or long-term solutions? Portland and Seattle are trying to answer this question in very visible ways by the way they work, the priorities they set, and the funding that is provided.

Portland, Oregon: A Place That Is Getting It Right

Truly achieving a triple bottom line approach to development, where economic, environmental, and social considerations are balanced as equal priorities, is a challenge few communities have accepted or even attempted. Portland, Oregon, with investments in downtown revitalization, light rail and other transportation modes, and a longer history than most cities in sustainability planning is widely known as a city "getting it right," but even Portland has a way to go to achieve the ideal balance of investments that will benefit the economic, environmental, and social health of all community members long-term. However, a long history of wise investments and decisions has set the right directions.

According to Susan Anderson, director of Portland's Bureau of Planning and Sustainability, Portland's early efforts, such as implementing a state-mandated Urban Growth Boundary to protect agricultural land, redirecting federal funds from a freeway to light rail, and replacing a former interstate with a new waterfront park, all set the stage for Portland to become a national leader in sustainability. Portland's city council has adopted a Sustainable City Government Partnership Policy ensuring sustainable practices citywide. Portland also is home to an extensive Green Building and Development Program and recently has released an interactive Green Design Atlas, identifying green building projects and sustainable sites all over the city (Green Design Atlas, 2013).

The greater Portland region is committed to developing regional and town centers, particularly along transit corridors. The regional governing body, Metro, was the first in the nation to use federal funds to acquire land for redevelopment adjacent to a light rail station ("TriMet Kicks Off . . . ," 2011). One contemporary example of Portland's transit investments is the Portland Mall, a 1.7-mile transit corridor that runs through six city districts and builds on an award-winning design implemented in the 1970s. The American Society of Landscape Architects Professional Awards Jury, when conferring the 2011 Award of Excellence for Portland's Transit Mall, stated, "They have taken a good idea and made it even better. It's a great expenditure of public money and so far ahead of what anyone else is doing. It's another example of Portland continuing to stay ahead. They were unafraid of taking out what didn't work and fixing it, which is difficult to do in cities" (American Society of Landscape Architects, 2013).

Portland is not content with where it is and is focused on where it could be. Dr. Janet Hammer, director of Portland State University's Initiative on Triple Bottom Line Development, led a series of focus groups with Portland-area municipal and county officials to explore to what extent jurisdictions are applying a "triple bottom line lens" for development and investment practices (Hammer, 2010). Hammer and her colleagues found that, despite expressed interest in doing so, few Portland-area jurisdictions employ an explicit triple bottom line approach to investment. One notable exception is the City of Lake Oswego, just south of Portland in Clackamas County, which uses a triple bottom line approach to inform selection of capital improvement projects: the Lake Oswego Capital Improvement Plan defines each project's priority using sustainability criteria (City of Lake Oswego, 2013).

Several initiatives in the City of Portland are making strides toward a triple bottom line approach. Portland International Airport's Futures Plan adopted sustainability as an overarching goal, including economic considerations such as supporting the role of the airport in the regional economy; environmental considerations such as avoiding, minimizing, or mitigating aircraft noise and greenhouse gas emissions; and social considerations such as addressing the airport's impacts on neighborhood livability (City of Portland Bureau of Planning and Sustainability, 2008).

A pilot program to improve the delivery of home energy upgrades, which eventually led to Clean Energy Works Oregon, is another example. Clean Energy Works Oregon is an energy conservation program that "creates green collar jobs that sustain families while helping the economy and environment" (Hammer, Babcock, Moosbrugger, 2012). Clean Energy Works Oregon boasts impressive triple bottom line statistics: high average wages and access to health insurance; average energy savings per home of over seven thousand kilowatt hours; and a commitment to employing underrepresented people in the industry, such as women and people of color (Hammer, Babcock, Moosbrugger, 2012, p. 20).

The Tualatin Valley Water District (TVWD), which supplies water to several communities immediately west of the City of Portland, is also committed to a triple bottom line approach, calling sustainability "a guiding force" for business operations. Sustainable practices are incorporated into all aspects of the TVWD. These practices include the collection of unwanted bicycle tire tubes from a local bicycle repair shop for use as sandbags to divert water when flushing out hydrants, preference for Oregon suppliers when purchasing materials, and a specialized Employee Recycling Benefit program allowing employees to recycle items they might not be able to recycle at home ("Taking the next step," 2006).

Portland is not just a research community but a learning one as well. It is leading the way in developing measures and methods to adopt and implement more triple bottom line approaches. This kind of investment strategy has been working for Portland for a long time—so much so, in fact, that it is becoming business as usual.

Seattle Still Soaring

Seattle, Washington, is considered a leader in sustainability—one that, according to Kent Portney, "stands at the top of virtually every list of sustainable cities" (2003, p. 193). Seattle's Office of Sustainability and Environment implements programs across government departments in areas such as food systems, urban forest management, and environmental sustainability innovation and research (Seattle Office of Sustainability and Environment, 2013). Sustainable Seattle, a nonprofit organization founded in the 1990s to spearhead sustainable practices throughout the city, complements government efforts through a series of neighborhood programs such as Green Blocks Blue Sound, a rain garden program; the Sustainable Neighbors Action Program, which encourages city residents to conserve energy; several sustainable business programs; and a Seattle Area Happiness Initiative, the first set of happiness indicators ever explored by any U.S. city (Sustainable Seattle, 2013).

Seattle Public Utilities (SPU), the city's utility provider, has implemented a series of innovative projects and programs, keeping the city on the forefront of environmental sustainability. Among these are a series of green storm-water infrastructure projects, incorporating natural drainage techniques across a variety of Seattle neighborhoods. In March 2013, Seattle Mayor Mike McGinn set a new goal for the city to manage seven hundred million gallons of storm water annually with existing and new green storm-water infrastructure. Upon the mayor's announcement, city council member Jean Godden expressed confidence that the "initiative will be another success in the City's groundbreaking environmental history" (McGinn, 2013). In 2012, SPU piloted a different type of project at the request of Seattle's city council: every-other-week garbage collection at four locations throughout the city. Based on the results of the pilot study, if implemented, the every-other-week collection is expected to divert several thousand tons of recyclables and food waste, increase efficiency, reduce operational costs, and reduce the number of trucks in neighborhoods (Seattle Public Utilities, 2013).

In addition to environmental sustainability efforts, Seattle also has made an explicit commitment to addressing race and social justice as part of government practice. In 2005 the city launched the Seattle Race and Social Justice Initiative (RSJI), with the stated goal of ending institutional racism in the city government, the first of its kind in any U.S. city. Glenn Harris, RSJI manager, describes how community activists in Seattle have been working to address racial disparities for many years, and the RSJI is looking to "expand on the history of that community organizing" (Race and Social Justice Initiative, 2013). The RSJI has three goals for the city: 1) to eliminate race-based inequities in our communities; 2) to strengthen how City government engages the community and provides services; and 3) to end racial disparities in City government, including a focus on both workforce and contracting equity initiatives. The initiative is being implemented at all levels of government and is making strides in an area of triple bottom line investment, social sustainability, that experts consider to be particularly lagging (Hammer, 2010).

So far, the RSJI has successfully initiated a Race and Social Justice Community Roundtable, which includes twenty-five community organizations such as the Arab American Community Coalition, the Minority Executive Directors' Coalition, the YMCA, and the Seattle Housing Authority, to name a few. The RSJI has increased the City of Seattle's contracts with women- and minority-owned businesses, expanded public engagement with historically underrepresented groups, and trained over seven thousand employees on ending institutional racism (RSJI, 2013). Gary Delgado, founder of the Applied Research Center and the Center for Third World Organizing calls Seattle's Race and Social Justice Initiative "an important model for the country because it involves community in fostering change in government" (RSJI, 2012, p. 6). RSJI proponents are not unaware of what they term "the enormity of the challenge" before them; however, the initiative's proven success and clear goals for future action are positioning the City of Seattle to be at the forefront of social equity and a truly inclusive place to live, work, and visit.

Finally, Seattle is working on enlarging the civic engagement of its community members by a strong focus on placemaking and the arts. Calling itself "City of Music," an initiative of Seattle's Office of Film and Music to include musicians, live music, and the business of music, Seattle has worked hard over the last few years to enhance and support music as a valuable and valued asset. After a 2002 economic impact study showed that the music industry had created more than twenty thousand jobs and generated a billion dollars in earnings and tax revenues, the city got serious about its efforts to support and expand the role that music played in the community and in the economy. The strategies include a public school component, festivals, increasing the number of venues, and even a musician home ownership program (Markusen and Gadwa, 2010).

Seattle is a community that has been questioning, including, and making things happen for decades. It provides a high quality of life, offers a robust economic climate, and is a gateway to Asia and the Pacific Rim. The community just seems to get smarter.

These three cities illustrate how an investment strategy goes beyond visioning or benchmarks. It is the process by which time, money, and personal resources are committed based on the community's shared values and commitment to the future. These cities are smart not because they scored the best or do everything perfectly, but rather because they have found ways to invest in their community that reflect where they are going and where they want to be in providing for people, place, and planet.

This chapter brought front and center the reality that we are faced with enormous challenges that need a wide range of capital investing. For every community that is not working well, there is another one that is doing well. By preventing problems, investing in balanced strategies, and staying the course to achieve long-term success, these communities and others are investing right the first time and reaping the rewards.

CHAPTER THREE

| Working Together

Americans don't always agree. We have strong feelings about athletic rivalries, political parties, and religious beliefs. There is one thing, however, that receives almost universal agreement: working together is better. In a survey, *What Will It Take? Making Headway on Our Most Wrenching Problems*, commissioned by the Pew Partnership for Civic Change in 2003, Americans said overwhelmingly (93 percent) that working together more closely on community problems leads to better results. When asked what would *most* improve the quality of life in the community, 40 percent said "working together" versus 14 percent who said "voting." These responses define our challenge—how to make working together business as usual.

The search for explanations of success for communities leads to the most predictable answer: groups of community members work together across sectoral lines. The expectation and the evidence is that people tackle the good times and bad more effectively together.

People join together on a myriad of projects, interests, and concerns. The world has witnessed enormous outpourings of support and generosity in times of crisis—floods, hurricanes, and tragedies of all types. The evidence is clear that people can link arms and join hands with the proper motivation. The key to community success, however, is the *habit* of working together, not the *incident* of working together. Democracy itself hinges on the ability of citizens to hang together and hang tough on the critical issues of the day.

Our communities no longer have the luxury of "going it alone." The complexity of the problems facing every corner of

...e world requires that people and organizations be willing and able to come together to craft strategies that are effective in good times and bad. In places where genuine joint action has occurred, results happen. These are not just pie-in-the-sky experiments, but rather gritty processes that bring citizens, educators, organizations, governments, and businesses together to create a different outcome. This chapter will look at the experiences of three communities—Chattanooga, Tennessee; Almena, Wisconsin; and Austin, Texas—which have figured out that their collective futures are tied to their ability to define problems and opportunities and organize themselves to take action—together. Was it always easy or fun? Absolutely not, as they would tell you. It was a necessity.

Communities have the capacity to meet important challenges directly and multilaterally if they organize themselves to act. However, rarely is it just structure that is the key to success. Americans choose to work together in different ways and for different reasons. However, it is clear that sustained efforts—those developed for a purpose and that work over time—must have a structure for working together that has broad implications for building social capital, creating unusual partnerships, and taking action on systemic issues, but also the public will to act.

Problems Cannot Be Solved Alone

Community organizations of all sizes have found that deep-seated community issues cannot be solved by one group alone. This has come as a surprise to some communities that have "siloed" or narrowly conceived their approaches to solutions. The seriousness of wicked problems, or merely everyday concerns, requires that groups recognize that most social problems are related, feed on one another, and cannot be addressed in isolation. For example, individuals who are making less than a living wage cannot afford decent housing in a safe neighborhood. These issues are all related; solving one of the issues without attention to the others has limited impact. Scarce resources require that communities use what is available in the best and most strategic ways. Sporadic interventions never solve systemic issues. The extent of our seemingly intractable problems, such as childhood poverty, illegal drugs, and lack of educational achievement, has caused commu-

nity organizations, business, and government to reach across organizational lines to form new alliances by necessity.

Community partnerships are motivated not only by self-
interest but also by common interests. At the national level, it is
not uncommon to see a number of organizations joining together
on issues that affect their individual organizations in different
ways. For example, the national debate on Head Start funding
brought together a wide range of organizations and individuals
who believed in the concept and felt that individuals, communities, and the nation would suffer without the program. Some of
these people had a personal stake in the issue—their job or the
agency depended on the appropriation; but others, although not
personally affected, had seen the positive results in the community and wanted to register their concerns about funding cuts. It
is important that community efforts of any magnitude include
and seek out not only the stakeholders who would logically be
included but also some unusual partners.

In brief, stakeholders are those people and organizations who
have an interest in changing a situation or an issue or in maintaining the status quo. They most often are the individuals, groups,
or organizations most affected by the causes or consequences of
an issue or situation (Bryson and Crosby, 1992, p. 65). However,
the most obvious stakeholders are not the only ones who have an
interest and are valuable to the process. Two other groups are
often overlooked: *knowledge holders* and *ripple-effect stakeholders*.

Knowledge Holders

Knowledge holders are people who have critical information
about the issue but may not be directly affected by the issue or
its consequences. They are different from "experts" in that their
role is not to tell the group what to do but to assist the group in
four ways:

1. Help group members present their concerns in more
    informed and precise ways

2. Increase access to information and level the playing field
    among stakeholders, some of whom may have greater
    positions of power

3. Raise controversial aspects of the issues that others may avoid

4. Help the group understand the systemic nature of the problem or opportunity and the interconnected parts

Knowledge holders create a more coherent view of the situation, which is not influenced by individual interests, and offer new information that breaks the stereotypes and frames of reference from which problems are too often viewed. The result is that knowledge holders can offer a new lens on the problem (Luke, 1998, p. 70).

Ripple-Effect Stakeholders

Ripple-effect stakeholders represent individuals or groups who feel the second or third impacts of an issue. Often the immediacy of an issue draws only the most affected or those who have the greatest concern. One of the effects of global warming is that the temperature of the Earth is increasing, causing changes in weather patterns and producing negative results in the form of floods, storms, and droughts. Therefore, it includes new ripple-effect stakeholders in the global warming discussion: insurance companies, for example. As one executive stated the case, global warming could "bankrupt the industry." It is certainly to their financial advantage to curb the causes of climate change that too often result in major property losses and human suffering (Luke, 1998, pp. 71–72).

All of this points to the need for communities to think broadly and inclusively as they come together to act on issues and opportunities that are important to their long-term future.

The best answers to our most wrenching issues or glorious opportunities come when there are collective deliberations, judgments, and ideas. Communities can create powerful scenarios and alternatives when these forces work together. There are several ways that the process of working together manifests itself. Sometimes it's informal—people just getting together to make something happen. More often than not, there are structures in place that allow a community to work more systematically toward common goals.

What Is Working Together?

Lesson number one about working together: never assume that a large group gathered in one place means that the individuals have worked together, will work together, or even might work together for any reason. Breakfast meetings with an outside visitor can usually draw a crowd, but assume nothing. Words such as *collaboration* and *partnership* are cast about regularly, but they mean more than a casual meeting or conversation. Working together is the ability of a group of people to develop a relationship of trust that will allow different perspectives to be heard and discussed with ultimate agreement to take action on the issue. That's more than a one-time gathering or an e-mail trail; it is a consistent, sustained relationship over time. Joining together requires trust and relationships as well as process and information. It is never an abstraction. What *might* work or *could* work or *should* work *only* works when people actually do something together.

The spectrum of working together usually includes some version of *cooperation, partnerships, coalition building, comprehensive community initiatives*, and *collaboration*. The most interesting new work has a larger scope and more and varied stakeholders resulting in better outcomes.

Cooperation is an inherent quality and characteristic that is common to all four of these organizing groups. It can be its own kind of relationship, but often that includes simply sharing information, jointly sponsoring events, or *not* blocking something.

Partnerships are quite common community structures formed between individuals, organizations, government agencies, and businesses that want to combine forces for results that match their own organization's best interests. In a survey done in 2001, *In It for the Long Haul: Community Partnerships Making a Difference* by the Pew Partnership for Civic Change (2001), with business, government, and nonprofit leaders in the two hundred largest cities, respondents cited a number of payoffs for partnerships beyond just the organizations involved or the specific issue addressed by the partnership:

1. Community partnerships raise visibility on local issues: it's hard for communities to solve problems they don't know about.

2. Partnerships can help communities set priorities for the allocation of resources.

3. Partnerships can unleash new talents and resources to address old and new problems and opportunities.

According to these leaders, partnership activities include information sharing and financial and in-kind support, but the critical function is tackling tough issues together. Leaders in all sectors saw this as essential to community success. Almost three-quarters of the business and nonprofit leaders and 90 percent of the government leaders said that they work with other groups in the community to address important issues. Although the partnerships take different forms and directions, the survey found that they clearly were forged around key issues. Specifically, nonprofit, government, and business leaders say that they communicate with different sectors on a regular basis; they provide direct services to community organizations beyond giving; create a *culture of caring* within their respective organizations with more than 50 percent of businesses and 40 percent of local governments giving employees paid time off to volunteer; and finally, all sectors say that they organize employee participation programs to help in the community through walk-a-thons, food drives, and so forth. Further, a clear majority of leaders serve on boards and invite representatives from the other sectors to serve on these boards. Partnerships, according to these executives, are alive and well and making a significant difference in the life of the community.

Coalitions are the third type of joint work strategy. Coalitions can be informal or formal arrangements that bring diverse groups together for joint action on a single issue or a set of issues. Members may have very different motivations for joining the coalition. Coalitions can be short-term or long-term, but throughout members retain their individual identities, goals, and missions. Coalitions are formed for joint action to advocate, to stop something, or to start something. Groups gather with a wide array of stakeholders around issues such as traffic control, crime, environmental concerns, corporate practices—you name it. For example, the Coalition to Stop Gun Violence has forty-four civic, professional, and religious organizational members, including the American Academy of Pediatrics, the Church of the Brethren, and the YWCA, and more than one hundred thousand individual members. A study on the sustainability of coalitions done for the Department of Health and Human Services in 2010 distinguished coalitions from other kinds of community organizations in three ways: 1) community coalitions can create collaborative capacity among diverse organizations; 2) they help communities build social capital; and 3) they are catalysts and agents for change around a range of issues. The study identified six characteristics that impact coalition functioning and effectiveness. These are the quality and consistency of leadership; a broad and engaged membership; a governance structure in place; processes for communication, decision making, and conflict resolution; a strategic vision for the coalition with complementary goals and objectives; and context and history within the community (U.S. Department of Health and Human Services, 2011).

Comprehensive Community Initiatives (CCI) is the fourth type of community process and organizational structure that has gained popularity in community development over the last two decades. It is a comprehensive strategy that empowers communities, neighborhoods, and community members to rely on each other, share information, and work on initiatives together. It emphasizes "community building" as both a means of neighborhood transformation and a principal outcome (Chaskin, 1999). CCIs do joint work on issues. They build and nurture their own capacity by bringing together all the available resources and skills to address common problems and meet opportunities. This approach builds social capital and gives communities more options for decision making. According to Chaskin (1999), community capacity building is

> . . . the interaction of human, organizational, and social capital existing within a given community that can be leveraged to solve collective problems and improve or maintain the well-being of a given community. It may operate through informal social processes and/or organized efforts by individuals, organizations, and the networks of associations among them and between them and the broader systems of which the community is a part. (p. 4)

A well-known example is the Dudley Street Neighborhood Initiative in Boston, which was formed to combat the negative influences on and treatment of the neighborhood. The Dudley

̣et Neighborhood literally had become a dumping ground for old cars, old furniture, and even old meat. Community members had little control over crime, arson, or dumping. Working with the city, the Riley Foundation, other local and national partners, and each other, the community found its voice and got its neighborhood back (Medoff and Sklar, 1994).

While places have had transformative experiences, many community-building efforts have fallen short of what an Aspen Institute report called "population-level changes." There have been individual improvements and even significant physical improvements, but the efforts have not moved the needle for the whole community. Expectations have exceeded accomplishments to date. But as John McKnight and Peter Block write in *The Abundant Community* (2010), "The starting point in every transformation is to think differently . . . . The culture of community is initiated by people who value each other's gifts and are seriously related to each other. It takes time, because serious relationships are based upon trust . . . ." (pp. 115 and 117). This makes a more comprehensive vision integral to revitalization efforts.

Collaboration is the fifth type of community structure. Collaboration means simply "to work together," but its larger definition has a clear set of requirements and assignments (Chrislip and Larson, 1994, p. 5). Both a process and a goal for community work, collaboration allows multiple stakeholders in a community to work together toward a common purpose, building on a community's resources, talents, and assets. Understandably, this basic definition is the first step in the journey. All too often, communities declare that this initiative or that is a collaboration; it rarely is at first glance. Collaboration is more often talked about than actually done! It is one of the hardest community efforts to organize and execute but can be the most effective. It is difficult for groups and individuals to "give up" the control necessary to form a genuine collaboration. Collaborations differ from partnerships and coalitions in that participating organizations actually merge their financial and organizational functions at some level. The sharing of resources, risks, and rewards is a foreign concept for those organizations that want to go it alone with the hope of having the spotlight shine on only their work and efforts. This strategy is fraught with difficulty, as the challenges communities face need a myriad of perspectives and stakeholders. That is what collaboration brings to the community table. Creating venues for joint work is not a one-size-fits-all endeavor. Certain circumstances require different methods of working together. Table 3.1 shows the stages of collaborative community work. Community efforts of any description work if, and only if, there is a sense that they will accomplish something bigger than the collective parts and if the parties involved and those in the larger community think the process is fair and inclusive.

How Joint Efforts Can Work Better

Community processes have characteristics all their own, but generally groups must address three phases: defining the problem, deciding on strategy, and taking action. These are rarely linear and are not easy to predict in terms of time or distinct blocks (Gray, 1989, p. 5). Problem definition requires that the group come to agreement on the problem or the opportunity that they are addressing. This "cards-on-the-table" stage is the critical period in which relationships and trust are built and ways of working agreed on. Other stakeholders are identified. It is critical that this early work create a clear view of the big picture, the commitment required, and the root causes of "the poblem behind the problem."

The second stage is framing the problem for action. Community members must be clear about the choices and trade-offs in solving the problem as well as the extent of the problem. Wicked problems rarely have a one-size-fits-all solution. Communities have to decide how the problem will be approached, what trade-offs can be accepted, and how the solution fits with their collective values. It includes data gathering, goal setting, and overall organization of the process: how it will work, who will do what, the expectations both from and of members, and how the group will proceed. Finally, the group has to act. This stage can cause groups the most consternation because it requires moving from talk to action. This period could require a different structure or a change in the working group. A new group or subcommittee may be charged with monitoring the progress and the process. Gray's phases have three clear messages: pay attention to process, involve and communicate with a broad range of stakeholders, and

Table 3.1. Assessing the Readiness for Joint Work

Cooperation	Partnership	Coalition Building	Comprehensive Community Initiatives	Collaboration
Information exchange	Information exchange	Information exchange	Information exchange	Information exchange
Support of each other's work	Shared purposes	Tactical purpose	Convening organization or network	Shared authority, risk, resources, and responsibility
Authority retained by parties	Coordination of programs or services	Shared outreach	Shared risk by parties	Comprehensive strategic planning
Goal: Increased efficiency of services and prevention of duplication	Limited joint planning	Coordinated planning	Comprehensive strategic planning	Clear communication channels
	Regular communication	Regular communication	Regular communications	Alteration of current activities
	Authority retained by parties	Authority retained by parties	Holistic approach	Noncompetitive environment
	Access to turf or span of authority	Short-term or long-term	Goal: To build local capacity by increasing human, social, built, political, environmental, and financial capital to address systemic problems	Creation of new operational structure
	Goal: Specific tasks accomplished that benefit from mutual expertise	Goal: To stop, start, continue, or improve a program, practice, or policy		Goal: Achievement of long-term, communitywide purpose or mission

Commitments of Time-Trust-Access

Source: This table draws on the work of Arthur T. Himmelman's "Communities Working Collaboratively for Change," in Margaret Herrman, ed., *Resolving Conflict: Strategies for Local Government* (Washington, D.C.: International City/County Management Association, 1994), pp. 27–47; and Suzanne W. Morse, *Building Collaborative Communities* (Charlottesville, Va.: Pew Partnership for Civic Change, 1996).

be clear up front about expectations and commitments (Gray 1989, pp. 86, 88–89).

Why Do Efforts Fail?

Too many community efforts fail or never get off the ground. Perhaps the one best-known reason is turf protection. People are afraid to join in, let go, and commit to activities over which they have limited control. Organizations often want to maintain their independence and keep their profile and good works high on the community's funding agenda. Joint work does not relieve an organization of its individual responsibilities or authority, but often it does create structures where the ultimate goal is a problem to be solved, not organizational survival. These efforts provide opportunities for people in jobs, agencies, and neighborhood groups to rethink how their organizational boundaries overlap and how they might be expanded to accomplish even more. Turf becomes less important as sustainable outcomes, economic vitality, and results take its place.

A second reason community efforts fail is that the fault lines of race, gender, ethnicity, socioeconomic difference, and age are barriers to genuine joint work. All too often, fault lines define the dynamics of any community effort. Community groups must know this, deal with it as a group, and move on. Although years of injustice or exclusion cannot be ignored, the new effort can build a forum and an opportunity for people from throughout the community to build trust, form relationships, and focus on issues of common concern. An example of this process in action took place at a community forum on youth violence in a small city. The discussion was held on the campus of a historically black college. As various participants began to speak about their fears and concerns for their children, the racial divide came down. It was clear from the discussion and exchange that everybody in the room was concerned about the safety of all young people; the concern was color-blind. The issue was about children—all children—not one race or the other.

A third barrier to working together is the "been there, done that, won't work" mentality that exists everywhere. It is particularly prevalent if a community has had a history of false starts or setbacks on prior collaborative ventures. In those cases, it is important to step back, know the pitfalls, and hear the various opinions on the reasons the effort won't work—and then dispel them! A community must build on the knowledge of prior efforts but not be strangled by them. Also it is likely that the big issues in a community have been big issues for a while. It is also likely that there are or have been ongoing efforts. With overlap almost ensured from one effort to another, groups must not only address the similarity but also acknowledge the new approach and the new people—the "what" and "who" that are making this effort different. Community efforts are supported greatly by a community structure for change. This must be a stable but fluid organizing structure that allows the joint work to go forward, provides supports and vehicles for getting new people involved, and provides a system of accountability. Usually these organizations operate with paid staff, volunteers, and an advisory group or board.

Finally, groups must be willing to spend ample time on the process of working together. When high-energy "can-do" people get in the same room, there is a tendency and considerable pressure to "just do something." Too-quick responses can be fraught with mistakes and missteps. No one is suggesting indefinite discussion, but there is a need for a structure and a process to help groups define the issues and their various solutions before leaping to a particular remedy.

Working Together Is a Necessity, Not a Luxury

A clear message from research and practice is that working together is not optional anymore. As demands for services exceed the available resources, circumstances require that communities maximize time, money, and effort. Working together is one of the most effective ways to do it. Also it is the only realistic way for wicked problems to get the attention and energy needed for sustained action. Placing a man on the moon required teamwork, an integration of knowledge, an investment of resources, and a clear vision of the goal—so does improving our communities.

The value of connecting with others in a community is one of the clear-cut principles of community success. While valued and visionary leaders are critical, it is the wisdom and energy that we hold collectively that is the value added. The three communities profiled here literally have written the playbook on how it is done and the results that have followed. Chattanooga is a city with a strong sense of where it is now and where it wants to go. A small town in Wisconsin, Almena, has defied the odds on the stabilization of small places. And finally, Austin, Texas, continues to reap the benefits of the work begun thirty years ago when community members decided—together—that they wanted a different future.

Chattanooga: A Real Joint Venture

When Chattanooga was selected as the site for the first Volkswagen manufacturing plant in America, no one was really surprised. Over the last forty years, Chattanooga has transformed itself into one of the most livable cities in America. When asked why Volkswagen was chosen over some very strong competitors, Stefan Jacoby said Chattanooga "is America at its best" (Volkswagen Group of America, 2008). But that hasn't always been the case.

In 1969 Chattanooga, Tennessee, received a "first" award for having the worst air quality in the nation. The air was filled with pollutants ranging from ozone to particulates to nitrous oxides emanating from the local munitions plant producing TNT. Chattanooga got itself in gear to respond. Working to accomplish more than the Environmental Protection Agency's recommended remedy, the City of Chattanooga and local groups set up a control board, initiated a public education campaign about pollution, and began to bring people together to talk about solutions. The effort worked, meeting air quality standards or exceeding them in five years (Adams and Parr, 1997, p. 47).

The success of this process sent a message throughout the community: they could work together not just on pollution but also on other issues. They set up a task force made up of people from across the community—elected officials, nonprofit leaders, businesspeople, and interested citizens—to look at the community's future. Chattanooga had been hard hit not only by the recession but also by a changing economic base that had closed many local factories or made them obsolete. In the early 1980s, the task force organized over sixty-five public meetings to sort through options. In the midst of these discussions, the task force visited Indianapolis, on the first of many road trips to get new ideas. That road trip produced a big idea: Chattanooga Venture. Indianapolis has had a decades-long history of strong business leadership on critical civic issues. Formally called the Greater Indianapolis Progress Committee, this group used community-wide task forces to address and define economic and social issues in the city. Chattanooga Venture was Chattanooga's version of the progress committee. Incorporated in 1984 and funded for a decade by the local Lyndhurst Foundation, Chattanooga Venture had almost three thousand participants in its heyday (Adams and Parr, 1997, pp. 41–42). The purpose was to bring Chattanoogans together to discuss and decide how the community would develop. Their motto was "to expedite positive community change through informed citizen involvement, to turn talk into action, to become the finest midsize city in America." Working on projects ranging from child care to historic preservation, the task forces began to look at every aspect of their shared community life. Dubbed the "Chattanooga Process," citizens in the community had found a new way to work. The collective good was always the goal; preventing problems and creating positive change were the priorities; and they learned from other communities.

Chattanooga Venture's first effort, Vision 2000, established forty goals for the city. The initiative resulted in more than two hundred projects and programs, created almost fourteen hundred jobs, leveraged a financial investment of $793 million, and included seventeen hundred people. The results of Chattanooga's efforts at collaboration and partnership have been impressive. By 1992 more than 90 percent of the goals had been completed or partially completed. The goals ranged from the development of the riverfront, to affordable housing, to advancement in human relations (Adams and Parr, 1997, pp. 47–48).

The Chattanooga story makes partnership and collaboration look easy in hindsight. It wasn't. Getting people to come together around issues requires skill, commitment, and a local group as mediator, cheerleader, coordinator, and visionary. They had all this in Chattanooga Venture. They set goals and used them as a road map to determine what the community needed and how those needs could be met. They put a spotlight on success and let citizens, business, government, and nonprofits do the work.

Was it all smooth sailing? "There were naysayers," says Mai Bell Hurley, former Chattanooga Vision chairperson. "Some people were suspicious of the process but very few." Chattanooga Venture itself was scaled down and eventually phased out, but with its initial work done, is part of the fabric of the community. In 1999 discussions on urban sprawl brought out twenty-five hundred people. Chattanooga has figured out that a commonsense, inclusive approach to real problems allows the best to be attained from all citizens, encourages new ideas to be discussed, and creates a constituency for change. Chattanooga has shown that change will come from a comprehensive process that incorporates ideas from the community and is supported by decisive citizens working together to make change (Best Management Practices Center of Excellence, 2007). Hurley says that the experience has changed the way Chattanooga does business forever. "Now almost any issue brings lots of people to community meetings. Now it's expected."

Since 2003 Chattanooga has continued to involve and engage community members in the betterment of the city and in improving the overall quality of life. With initiatives to improve schools, create jobs, and protect low-income residents, Chattanooga has created an environment where all people feel relevant and have the ability to influence the direction of the community. Many of the community organizations in Chattanooga are relatively new but have managed to positively influence the city during their short life spans. Others served the region well before 2003, but their unwavering commitment to the role of the citizens still fuels the programs and has allowed for new projects and "victories" in recent years. In short, Chattanooga has maintained an open and honest environment. There are new organizations in place for community members' voices to be heard, and they still value working together.

Chattanooga today, thirty years later, shows a transformation in place and culture. There are still problems to be sure, but its physical appearance, population, and economic health are all quite different. The downtown has been rejuvenated; the waterfront has had a multimillion-dollar revitalization; many more projects are on the drawing board; but most important, the habit of working together is evident. Communities create their map for change in different ways. Chattanooga learned from Indianapolis, Charlotte, and others, and in turn, many have learned from Chattanooga. One of the smartest decisions that Chattanooga made in the last thirty years was to create a structure that facilitated the citizens' ability to work together to address their common problems and opportunities. This really is America at its best.

Small and Together Still Works: Almena, Wisconsin

Rural areas seem to have felt the impact of suburbanization, a changing economy, and an out-migration of young people in ways that even some of the hardest-hit urban areas have not. These places have seen the absorption of the family farm into conglomerates; extracting industries such as coal and logging on the decline; and once-thriving downtowns circumvented by interstates. In some places, it is tough to be small. Communities sometimes see partnerships as the avenue of last resort and the only avenue out of their current situation.

This was the scenario in Almena, Wisconsin, almost thirty years ago. The village of Almena, located in west central Wisconsin, is representative of the pressures facing rural areas nationwide and farming communities in particular. In the 1980s the agricultural depression hit Almena hard, as did increasing competition from regional commercial and retail centers. The village lost its largest employer, Koser Silo, and with it several Main Street stores, including the only grocery store. Even though the community remained hopeful that things would turn around, there were few positive signs. Almena is a German settlement that reflects the values and attributes of its ancestors: toughness, stubbornness, and realism. This was a tough situation and they knew it. Amid the downturn, the community decided to celebrate its centennial in 1987 with a weekend-long series of events. Citizens worked long hours to research local history, organize activities, and get the word out. The celebration brought out hundreds of people and produced two very important results: first, the successful organization and execution of the event showed the community that they could do something together; and second, they raised money. The Commercial Club (their chamber of commerce) decided to earmark $25,000 of the profits from the centennial to attract industry to Almena. They approached a regional community development organization, Impact Seven, for assistance. The strategic alliance with Impact Seven proved to be the catalyst and the guidance that the village needed. Impact Seven had been working in the region and the state since 1970. Its experience in encouraging economic development, job creation, and business expansion, particularly for low-income people, was just what Almena needed. Their mutual interests brought the two together in a public-private partnership that included the Commercial Club, village administration, other local organizations such as civic clubs, and later, Almena Business Development Corporation. The village groups joined together and pooled resources with one goal in mind—the revitalization of Almena. Rather than chase a myriad of single projects, the group decided that all resources would be focused on the Almena Idea. The first step in the process was to identify the needs and priorities of the community. Over a three-day period of evening meetings and through a questionnaire, citizens were able to articulate their visions to bring Almena back. The overall consensus was that the village had to have more commerce and industry in town. Their focus was to be on community redevelopment, which included jobs and the revitalization of the community. The Almena Idea comprised three key parts: marketing, infrastructure improvements, and financial assistance to firms interested in locating to Almena or expanding existing operations. To oversee these tasks, the Almena Business Development Corporation was created in 1990.

Using state and federal loans and grants and tax incremental financing, the community created two industrial development parks (116 acres) to be used for business diversification and job creation. They began a marketing program to make the Almena business location opportunity known to business and industry. Their first bite was an industrial development contract with the Farmers Home Administration in 1991 for the expansion of two businesses. That same year, the first new business arrived: L & M Gazebos, which added ten new jobs at peak production. Each subsequent year, more pieces began to fall into place. Money was raised for downtown revitalization, infrastructure improvements were made at the industrial park, and ground was broken on the Greater Wisconsin Business Center. In 1992 four additional businesses were added, and with them came twenty-five new jobs. In 1994 (just four years after the process began), the village established a Head Start program with six new jobs and added four other corporations, bringing thirty-five more jobs. A local bank razed a dilapidated building to create a new town square. A grant from the National Endowment for the Arts and matching local support allowed for the development of a downtown revitalization plan and the re-awakening of Main Street. Further, the village planted trees, created small businesses, and even developed a trailhead for a local snowmobile–all-terrain vehicle trail, called Cattail. The Almena Elementary School not only was saved, it was expanded. A facility for low-income seniors was opened. Impact Seven moved its offices to Almena.

Things slowed down a bit in Almena during the economic downturn of 2007. The population has leveled out at about seven hundred people. But the seeds that were sown decades ago are continuing to show results. The Business Development Corporation is stronger and has more experience working with and recruiting new businesses. Likewise, the Village Board and Almena Community Club are more involved in economic vitality and are working together on a new RV park. More single-family homes are being built, and the school is scaling back up to offer more grades again. Social capital is on the rise. Almena Fun Days still draw together partners such as the Veterans of Foreign Wars, service clubs, and community churches. But perhaps the most telling example of how things are going is illustrated through the organization and implementation of spring clean-up days. The aftermath of Wisconsin winter weather leaves a variety of chores to do to get the village ready for the spring season. The village could just hire people to sweep the debris, clean the benches, and clear the trails, but they do it themselves. An organizing committee assigns civic groups, church fellowships, and a variety of local organizations for one area of the clean-up, respectively, and groups follow through. This is a village that knows how to get things done—together.

The innovation of the Almena Idea, however, was due in part to the work of the "irritant," or organizer, in the turnaround. Almena needed that grain of sand which Impact Seven brought to the partnership to change the habits, attitudes, and practices that had become embedded in the community. In some situations, the loss of a major employer can galvanize a community to act. However, the cumulative losses are sometimes too much for a small community. A string of small-business losses coupled with the loss of a major employer creates a gloom-and-doom scenario. Failure becomes a self-fulfilling prophecy, fueled by cynicism, skepticism, and doubt. This is where the innovation of a strategic alliance is so necessary. In Almena's case, the alliance was composed of a community development corporation, Impact Seven; a local development corporation; community members; and the village itself. Each party played a critical role in changing attitudes and creating one success at a time.

Austin: It Is Not Weird, It Is Working

In 2000 when an Austin Community College librarian, Red Was-senich, coined the phrase "Keep Austin Weird," little did he know he would set off a storm of commercial enterprises, websites, and international envy! Austin has been so successful as a leader in the technology and research field that most everyone wants to know how being weird figures into success. On the surface, Austin is thought to be "weird" because of its concentration of noncon-formist people and ideas, but it was also weird more than three decades ago when it did something that many communities could not have done on a bet—worked together.

Opportunities are born as well as problems solved when people can come together. In the early 1980s, Austin, Texas, was a stable state capital with a large university in its midst. Public sector institutions, including state, county, city, and the University of Texas, were the major employers. The stability of these organizations kept Austin's economy on an even keel. In the early 1960s, branch plants of several major firms, such as IBM, Texas Instruments, Lockheed, and Intel, and Defense Department contracts brought good jobs to the area. The Austin of the 1980s was essentially a city of important pieces, but not a big picture. There were some real drawbacks in the way the city operated: some in the city were hostile to growth; the university was a presence, not a player; the nucleus of technology firms was small; and the mind-set was oil and gas (Henton, Melville, and Walesh, 1997, p. 43).

According to former mayor Kirk Watson, Austin's history can be tracked by three transitions. The first period, he says, is that of the original design of the city. There are basically four dimensions: the river on one side, capitol hill on another, and creeks on the east and west. It was clear even from the early days that "capitol hill" and "college hill" would be prominent in the city's development. (The capitol dome and the tower of the University of Texas form a straight line.) The second transitional period came during the 1940s, says Watson, when the Colorado River was finally and successfully dammed. This brought increased electrical power to the area and allowed for growth and development along the river's edge. During this period, however, there was an implied commitment that the business of Austin would be state government and higher education. There was not a concerted push for new industry.

The third transition began in 1983 and changed the economic landscape in Austin forever. With a light-manufacturing sector and a highly educated workforce in place, the community was ready to move to the next step. The chamber of commerce, the governor's office, the University of Texas, businesspeople, citizens, and local leaders throughout the community developed a strategy to combat the declining economy and falling oil prices. The strategy focused on technology, and the goal was to land one of the biggest economic prizes of the decade—the Microelectronics Computer Technology Consortium (MCC). The winning community could look forward to significant research investment in laboratories and research facilities, an influx of scientists and technicians, and a big ticket to the prosperity of the twenty-first century. Austin found itself in competition with Research Triangle Park in North Carolina, San Diego, California, and other larger areas; in total, fifty-seven cities were in the competition. The working group of businesspeople, college professors, progressive government leaders, and interested citizens met every morning for months to hone the strategy and to identify those elements of Austin that would make it more attractive than the competition. They emphasized the research capacity at the University of Texas, the educational system, cultural amenities, and the quality of life—anything that would set Austin apart. This process and their successful application showed the community not only that leadership across sectors could work together, but also that this effort could change the future of the region. In 1988, the city also won the SEMATECH competition and became home to a consortium of semiconductor manufacturers. That prize resulted in more development locally. The University of Texas developed a research park and endowed thirty-two chairs in engineering and natural sciences (Henton, Melville, and Walesh, 1997, p. 43).

So where does modern-day Austin get its kick? Watson believes it was neither coincidence nor blind luck—the pieces were all in place. As he tells it, "It is not coincidence that Austin calls itself the 'live-music capital of the world.' The creativity that helped fuel the MCC and SEMATECH successes fuels the music industry." He gives example after example of the building blocks—such as large stores of intellectual capital; an emphasis on the environment and recreation; and the value of diversity of people, opinions, and ideas—that created the foundation which allowed Austin to fulfill its natural instincts for a creative economy.

There are many other places with state capitals and major universities that aren't doing nearly so well. In a series of articles for the *Austin-American Statesman*, two reporters began to search for some answers. First, they found that Austin has created an environment where people feel comfortable pushing the envelope. It is an open community that welcomes creative energy of all types, from technology to dance. Second, it is a community of ideas. Diversity of opinions is welcome. A third factor, they say, is Austin's openness to immigrants and newcomers. They bring with them expertise, a work ethic, and new ways of looking at the world. The authors quote William Frey, who contends, "They [immigrants] revitalize the regions they move to and enrich them culturally with their tastes in music, food, and entertainment. The regions that do not attract [immigrants] have often experienced prolonged economic decline, or they lack the natural or cultural amenities that many immigrants seek" (Lisheron and Bishop, 2002).

Fast-forward thirty years and Austin's technology sector contributes $21 billion annually to the local economy. Over the next five years, the tech sector is expected to grow and will likely hire ten thousand more people (*Wall Street Journal*, 2013). There are still challenges and opportunities. Meeting the demand for a skilled workforce in the larger region has been a continuing challenge for Austin and will likely continue to be. Poverty and its related problems plague too many people in the community. The public schools are a continuing concern. However, Austin has the potential, the wherewithal, and the responsibility to lift all boats. It has done so before. Austin knows what it takes to be a "creative" community. Take the issue of bats, for example. While many communities would think about ways to rid the community of these flying mammals, Austin was able to capitalize on its huge colony of Mexican free-tailed bats by transforming the city's least-popular inhabitants into a resource based on a natural phenomenon that brings in over a hundred thousand people per year. Austin chose to embrace a potential menace as an economic driver. An educational campaign launched by Dr. Merlin Tuttle, founder and then president of Bat Conservation International, with local leaders and the media about bats and their value to the ecosystem turned community fear into community appreciation. Bats now bring in an estimated $12 million in ecotourism dollars each year and consume fifteen tons of insects, according to Ryser and Popovici (1999). Boasting the world's largest urban bat colony, Austin now has a minor league ice hockey team called the Austin Ice Bats, numerous bat symbols strategically located around the city, and a host of educational programs around bats that cater to locals as well as tourists. Not only have Austin and nearby San Antonio capitalized on bats, but the Texas Department of Transportation now considers ways to adapt new bridges and roadways across the state to be bat friendly.

What has evolved in Austin is a culture of progress that invites, encourages, and supports working together in a creative, innovative, and open environment. They are meeting the challenges of the future by engaging people and their talents. Their SpeakUp-Austin initiative actively seeks community members' ideas on everything from bike hubs to budgeting. Operating online, the initiative has had a good response and is finding new ways to get the voice of community members heard on a range of issues. The community comes together in Austin through festivals, outdoor recreation, and even bats. Weird could be another word for working together works.

Working Together Is the Name of the Game in the New Economy

These community illustrations examine very different issues, ranging from the environment to economic development to small-town revitalization, but they all highlight key decisions by these communities to create a new direction. There are some commonalities, however, among the three. In each case, there was an outside challenge or opportunity that prompted action. Chattanooga had economic and environmental challenges to address; Almena had a declining rural economy; and Austin had an incredible economic development opportunity. The point is that change is inevitable. If communities are organized to respond, adapt, and meet it head-on, they are way ahead of the game. If they can do it collectively, they are calling the game.

Community efforts such as partnership, coalitions, and collaboration allow organizations and whole communities the opportunity to imagine different options, think outside traditional lines, and get more done. "The ultimate achievement for a collaboration is not that it worked well among the collaborators, although that is highly desired. Rather, it is that outcomes beneficial to a community are brought about" (Council on Foundations, 1995, p. 9).

Communities and organizations will encounter predictable rough spots, setbacks, and problems as they work together. However, amid the need to tidy the process, establish norms, and ensure accountability from all the parties, it is important to realize that community endeavors are not technical processes—they are, first and foremost, human endeavors. They are also democratic practices—challenged by the choices that must be made and the actions taken. Wynton Marsalis provides a metaphorical framework for understanding the challenges and opportunities of working together in his description of jazz. "Jazz is the music of conversation," says Marsalis, and that is what you need in a democracy. A truly American art form, jazz has its roots in homes, clubs, churches, and communities. Modern-day jazz has evolved from pick-up music to a clear set of sounds and styles. Marsalis describes jazz as a social invention. There are clear parallels between his description of jazz and understanding how communities do their work (Scherman, 1996, pp. 29–36). Marsalis says that jazz must have the attributes of music and other things. There must be a willingness to play with a theme or concept, for example. In the language of community, it is the time when a problem or opportunity is defined. Jazz invites participation and reaction; so do collaboration and partnership. And jazz has an inherent respect for individuality. "Playing jazz," says Marsalis, "means learning how to reconcile differences, even when they're Opposites . . . Jazz teaches you how to have dialogue with integrity" (Scherman, 1996, p. 29).

The process of working together across sectors must encompass human qualities as well as strategic ones. The jazz metaphor provides a straightforward preview of what can be expected and what groups must do. The ability to work together comes when citizens realize for themselves that working together is not only better, it is the only real option for creating change.

The communities profiled here have a sense of not only their own efficacy but also their own values—they know the language of community. These places had an idea of the kind of community they wanted and organized themselves to achieve it. This does not just happen on its own. It takes years of building trust, relationships, and a system of norms and expectations.

CHAPTER FOUR

Building on Community Strengths

Mingo County used what they had to make what they wanted— more jobs. Located in the southwestern corner of West Virginia, Mingo County is home to the Williamson Coal Field and its seventeen remaining coal camps. Mingo County, like many places where coal was mined and plentiful, has seen a decline in the jobs associated with the industry. At one time considered one of the top mining areas in the southeastern United States, 30 percent of the workforce still works in the mines. Thinner and less accessible seams and more affordable gasoline has lessened demand for the black gold. That change was partly mitigated at the turn of the twenty-first century as one of West Virginia's most plentiful and available resources—cold mine water discharge from abandoned coal mines—was used to literally spawn a new industry.

In 2000 the Mingo County Redevelopment Authority launched the aquaculture industry in West Virginia when it opened its first hatchery for the highly popular restaurant fish Artic char. The water from the mines is aerated and flows via gravity to the fish tanks. The demand and need were illustrated perfectly. Area workers needed an option in addition to mining, and the United States needed to meet the larger demand for seafood with local suppliers. Rated as the second largest seafood market in the world, we only produced a tenth of the supply domestically in 2000. To say that this was an unusual marriage of one industry to another is an understatement. For now the fish industry is transitioning, but not the idea and the lesson of the "adaptive reuse" of local assets.

All too frequently, community members, local organizations, and government officials see a community's needs and weaknesses: the silhouette of a community rather than the whole picture. Media, political hopefuls, and the usual naysayers too often paint a portrait of communities and neighborhoods based on statistics, impressions, and labels. For residents bombarded with the strains of everyday living, it is hard to separate the positives from the negatives and understand how and where to begin a change strategy. Distressed communities are defined by their challenges, not by their possibilities. Places have "half-full, half empty" complexes, just like individuals.

Despite the impact of changing markets, the outsourcing of once mainstay goods and services, and a communication explosion that allows work to be done in every corner of the earth, some communities are flourishing and others are finding their footing after setbacks and disappointments. Populations are growing again, and localities and places are valued for their quality of life and high social capital. All of this works in favor of new perspectives on work, corporate site selection, and living decisions. This positive development is generated by a change in mind-set—one that leads with what is present, not what is absent, and sees possibilities beyond the status quo.

On streets, in neighborhoods, and in whole towns and cities, there are signs of hope and reinvigoration. In some places, the downward spiral not only has stopped but actually has reversed. There are isolated cases of one new business or a revitalized area being the stimulus, but more often than not community members point to a new feeling or atmosphere that is positive and proactive about the future built on a combination of things. No longer content to let things just happen, community members are joining together to build relationships and look for answers within. These communities have places and opportunities for information to be exchanged; they encourage residents to deliberate and discuss goals and expectations; they solicit and value advice and best practice beyond their boundaries; and, last but not least, they refocus on the unique qualities, buildings, historical context, and cultural and natural amenities of their area. In other words, they leverage their assets.

Asset-Driven Approach to Community Development

The asset-based approach to community development introduced two decades ago forever altered the strategies and the mind-set that practitioners, planners, health professionals, and scholars use to approach community development. More important, it gave citizens new tools and perspectives to restore and revitalize their communities. Identifying assets in very challenged places can give depressed places anchors for development that can help increase their competitive edge and build the momentum to address immediate problems more effectively. Focusing on assets when the statistics are overwhelmingly negative and the long-term outlook bleak create new possibilities for residents and the organizations that work with them. The practical nature of the asset-based approach was identified early in the community research and observation done by Kretzmann and McKnight (1993) on the south side of Chicago, an area known to have significant social and economic challenges. The key to community regeneration "is to locate all the available assets in the local community, to begin connecting them with one another in ways that multiply their power and effectiveness, and to begin to harness local institutions that are not yet available for local development purposes" (Kretzmann and McKnight, 1993, pp. 5–6). The concept is being used not only for community and economic development but also to improve health outcomes. An article in *Pediatrics* profiled ways that the asset-based approach could be used to improve public health. One particular example is illustrative of the power of the concept for community problem solving. One of the pediatric residents participating in an asset-based training at the University of California, Davis School of Medicine noticed that there were an unusually high number of dog bites on children coming into the emergency room. After inquiring, the resident discovered that the children who had been bitten had little or no experience with dogs. Using asset-mapping techniques, she discovered people in the community who could lead and participate in a dog safety program for children (Pan, Littlefield, Valladolid, Tapping, and West, 2005, p. 115).

Identifying community assets begins by challenging people to think about their own lives and surroundings differently. Each person has gifts, skills, and capacities that communities need.

Young people, seniors, the unemployed, the disabled—all have incredible assets to bring to our communities. We need them and they need the community. Shifting the focus to assets and not deficits is not a low-income strategy; it is one that can benefit every community in untold ways.

Community members, organizations, and institutions discover synergies as assets are identified, mapped, and repurposed for new opportunities, new functions, and value-added impact. Kretzmann and McKnight and their colleagues at the Asset-Based Community Development Institute at Northwestern University have developed a number of survey instruments to gather asset information about individuals, associations, organizations, and institutions. Developing an asset map is not an academic exercise, but rather is an interactive way to connect individuals to their own talents and to the talents of others that could benefit the community, as well as gauge the depth and breadth of existing associations and organizations. In a nutshell, asset mapping allows a community to know itself and imagine a different set of relationships, resources, and interactions that could be leveraged on its own behalf. In other words, it is not just a map!

Knowing and building from assets rather than from deficits is both a compelling strategy and a practical approach to achieving better results in neighborhoods (Kretzmann and McKnight, 1993, p. 25). While the process is not a substitute for strategic community investing, research has shown that communities cannot be revitalized without the gifts, talents, and tenacity of the people in the neighborhood and that outside experts often ignore the wealth of talent and possibility embedded in the community. Further, the asset approach is often a bridge to the community fault lines of levels of participation, race, gender, and equity identified by Green and Haines (2002, pp. 27–30). The concept has spawned a range of ideas and interests that fall under monikers such as place-based economies, ecotourism, heritage tourism, and the like. Crisis prevents people, planners, and policymakers in communities from doing what Rosabeth Moss Kanter (2000) calls "kaleidoscope thinking." Kanter describes this as the ability to construct patterns from the information available and then manipulate them to form different patterns. This new lens allows people to see new solutions and new possibilities.

Twenty years later, amid budget cuts, sequesters, and political divides, the wisdom of asset-based community development holds firm. The concept includes personal or associational assets as well as the built and cultural environments. Communities of all sizes are cataloguing what they have already in place and how these people, places, and things can improve their quality of life and economic opportunities. However, despite the power of the concept, community leaders often are perplexed when trying to identify the assets to leverage and the ones to pass by. The dilemma runs the gamut from deciding which buildings to restore, to what asset-based focus fits with the culture, history, and personality of the community, to which investments best connect natural resources to the built environment. Most communities do not have unlimited resources or time to test-market an idea or conduct sophisticated economic forecasts. They need strategies to engage citizens and nonprofit, public, and corporate partners in thinking about the assets at hand and how those can be leveraged to improve the quality of life and economic impact.

Developing a Community from Within

Research has shown that successful communities are those that foster positive relationships with their residents. Communities will be rebuilt and empowered when effective public policies are joined with renewed efforts to strengthen all capital investments within communities, but particularly social capital. Efforts to build capital from assets of all types require that there be permanent, sustainable organizations in communities, which serve as anchors for overall development efforts. More and more foundations, governments, nonprofits, and businesses have realized the power of effective community-based organizations which believe that people—all people—bring assets to the community table that are valuable and critical to overall community success. They just need to be tapped. These organizations are key to the community infrastructure needed to make progress, as Brugmann (2009) reminds us.

Revitalization comes from a combination of factors, but community building through asset-based development and relationship building are essential parts of the equation. Angela Glover

Blackwell, president and chief executive officer of PolicyLink in Oakland, California, defines community building as "continuous, self-renewing efforts by residents, community leaders and professionals engaged in collective action aimed at problem-solving and enrichment that result in improved lives and greater equity and produce new or strengthened institutions, organizations, relationships, and new standards and expectations for life in the community" (Blackwell, 2005, n.p.). Community building is about the necessary actions and activities that happen every day between and among community members. Robert Sampson's research shows that some communities are safer than others because of the fabric of the community and residential stability. Studies controlled for poverty and other negative community factors show that crime hits communities hardest when teenagers are left unsupervised, where there are sparse relationships or anonymity among residents, and where there is low participation or few connections in local activities (Sampson, 1999).

Sustainable community development happens when the public is engaged, not just persuaded, and when the community has a sense of what it has in itself—its inner strengths. In many low-income communities, what is most visible is what's missing (grocery stores, neighborhood retail stores, and well-kept homes and apartments) and the bad things that are there (too many unemployed people on street corners, too many abandoned buildings and cars, and too much glass on the playgrounds). Amid those two stark scenarios are people, organizations, associations, institutions that have ideas, capacity, and the will to make things better and a natural and built environment as a foundation. The natural assets of place—such as weather, terrain, traditions, and natural resources—cannot be bought or built, but they can be harnessed and shaped for advantage. Pretty's (1998) discussion of the impact of land and agriculture on the regeneration of rural areas in Europe provides a series of examples of ways that local land and culture work in tandem to create an asset.

This approach begins with identifying assets and connecting them. Creating a community's ability to change its own future can take several approaches. It can focus largely on organizations and individuals; it can focus on effective connections and shared values; and it can focus on civic participation and engagement.

This is exactly the scene that played out in the Broadmoor neighborhood as community members set about finding a way to involve the community in maintaining their community and, ultimately, building a new future on the assets they had all along.

Broadmoor: Much More Than a Dot

It is widely acknowledged that disaster often brings communities together, bridges long-standing divides, and provides ample opportunity to improve what were seemingly intractable community problems. When Hurricane Katrina plowed through New Orleans in late 2005, it left residents with physically ruined neighborhoods, permanently displacing some and posing extremely difficult and emotional questions for city, community, and neighborhood leaders. For example, should every neighborhood be rebuilt or should planning reconstruction efforts be concentrated on the most viable and least flood-prone areas of the city? Such questions were answered in starkly contrasting terms by Mayor Nagin's administration, federal relief agencies, and neighborhood leaders in the aftermath of the storm.

Placing a dot on a map for future development plans without prior communication with affected neighborhoods predictably will incite vehement protests from residents—this is a basic and early lesson for students of urban planning and public administration. Yet the Nagin administration did exactly that in New Orleans, placing green dots upon a number of neighborhoods throughout the city early in 2006. A four-month timeline to "prove their viability" was set before the plans became finalized and those communities were written off as dead. The Broadmoor neighborhood was "green-dotted" and responded with an aggressive and comprehensive neighborhood organizing effort. In the years since Katrina, its efforts and successes have been widely recognized, demonstrating the power of a tenacious group of citizens who stepped into the leadership void left by all levels of government. The assimilation of a broad community coalition, strategic partnerships built far beyond the city, and smart leveraging of resources turned the neighborhood around and holds a number of lessons for other communities, most not consumed by crisis management.

Broadmoor is one of the lowest-lying areas of New Orleans and was drained beginning in the late nineteenth century, growing to over seven thousand residents by 2000. Pre-Katrina, many observers claimed it was representative of New Orleans's overall demographics given its racial and socioeconomic diversity. The Broadmoor Improvement Association (BIA) represented the neighborhood's interests and had an active past, recognized as the first neighborhood association in the country to sue a realty company over racial blockbusting practices.

Faced not only with the task of rehabilitating and inhabiting severely damaged homes (100 percent of the housing units in Broadmoor sustained major to severe damage in Katrina), Broadmoor residents also faced the task of organizing *against* the city's planning efforts. With no time to lose, a core group of neighborhood organizers sprang into action by organizing over one hundred community meetings during four months to painstakingly strategize and plan for both the return of dispersed residents and future planning of the neighborhood that was a viable alternative to the city's plan. A resident marketing professional branded their efforts, "Broadmoor Lives"; planning committees focused on topics such as economic development, schools, and transportation; and when meetings turned toward gripe sessions, organizers directly challenged their neighbors to organize a subcommittee, develop a coherent policy, and work toward a real solution. No longer intent on only dodging the ominous green dot, the neighborhood decided to rebuild and become stronger than ever. Their efforts solidified in the establishment of the Broadmoor Development Corporation (BDC) by the end of 2006, focused especially on housing recovery and stability.

While neighborhood residents built momentum to reclaim their neighborhood from devastation and bureaucratic blundering, the partnerships they built within the community and beyond led to the development of significant civic capacity. Broadmoor's faith institutions proved to be nimble, proactive partners in meeting basic needs such as food, water, and cleaning supplies in the absence of promised help by slow-moving state and national government agencies. A Harvard professor with connections to Broadmoor led a team of students who tactfully assisted in fine-tuning the neighborhood's vision of future rebuilding into the language of the best current practices of urban planning and hazard mitigation. Partnerships were also built with Bard College, Notre Dame, and MIT, providing additional help and energetic bodies on the streets to conduct intensive house-by-house data-gathering efforts (Scott, 2008).

Scouring national legislation passing through Congress and the Senate at that time, the Harvard professor also brought the grim news to the community that very few funds actually would be allocated to rebuilding the city. As this realization set in, the Broadmoor community reached far outside of the city to develop partnerships with national organizations. Through a fortuitous turn of events, the Clinton Global Initiative eventually awarded the BIA $5 million. These funds leveraged more capital and investments that rebuilt basic civic institutions such as schools and libraries in Broadmoor within three years of the disaster.

Five years after Katrina, Broadmoor residents had achieved many of the goals they set after the disaster:

- Rebuilding anchor educational institutions
- Implementing physical streetscape improvements throughout the district
- Repopulating
- Building notable community capacity around new institutions such as the BDC
- Attracting over $127 million in investments
- Strengthening community bonds that breached race and income differences through the shared experiences of tragedy and rebuilding

Many challenges remain in Broadmoor that were present pre-Katrina such as low educational achievement and the debilitating effects of blighted properties on reinvestment and community development. Incorporating the grassroots energy and strong momentum that spurred Broadmoor's comeback into newly established community institutions is an ongoing challenge. The identification of a catalyst for community revitalization in the absence of unifying external threats remains one of the biggest questions for other communities seeking to reinvigorate civic capacity and address longstanding issues (Seidman, 2013).

Assets Come in All Sizes

As the country has become more urbanized, more and more small towns and villages are left in precarious situations. There is an outflow of jobs, young people, and amenities as residents follow work opportunities or a desired quality of life. Rural areas are hard hit by all the big-city problems such as poverty, illegal drugs, and unemployment with fewer services to assist. Amid the bad statistics and the low expectations are small towns and villages such as Colquitt, Georgia, and Chimney Rock, North Carolina, that have changed their own odds for success. They had leadership that spurred efforts along, and they used their local assets to build a bright future.

Colquitt, Georgia: We've Got a Story to Tell—Our Own

Sometimes the problem is not the new economy or offshoring or even technology, sometimes it is just years of lack of investment, racial discrimination, exclusive power structures, or simply the population shifts that come with rural-to-urban migration. Colquitt, Georgia, had a little of all of this in 1990. What does the ninth-poorest congressional district in the United States have to tell others? Lots of things. And they do it several times a year to packed audiences.

Colquitt, Georgia, is in the southwest corner of Georgia, fifty miles from Tallahassee, Florida, and from Dothan, Alabama. In 1990 a local businesswoman, Joy Jinks, heard about the idea of a community play while attending a creativity conference in New York City. The presenter, Richard Geer, was looking for a place to try out his idea. Jinks was intrigued and talked with him further about Colquitt. She and other community leaders originally had wanted to do a historical play about the area, but the story idea was very appealing. The volunteers at the local arts council, where Jinks was a volunteer, thought so too. The idea was powerfully simple: a community records its oral history and produces the stories in a play, citizens in the community are the actors, and the people in the community connect personally in new ways. A group of volunteers batted around the idea and thought it just might work. Geer came down from Chicago to begin the planning process. Not everyone in the broader community was sold, however, remembers Karen Kimbrel, former executive director of the arts council and one of the movers and shakers who made it happen. "We had to do some consensus building. Some people were afraid it would stir up racial discord or political problems or wake up old ghosts." Others thought the "outsiders" might steal their stories for their own benefit. However, the working group pushed on and tried to allay the fears by assuring the community that it was the "trustee of its stories." A small grant from the Georgia Humanities Council provided funds for a local team to begin to gather the oral histories. More than a thousand stories have been collected since 1992. The play, named Swamp Gravy after a dish made from fried-fish remnants and vegetables to stretch a meal, was beginning to take shape. A professional script-writer wrote the scripts based on the oral histories, volunteers made the sets and costumes, a hundred volunteer performers played the parts, and the local elementary school lent its auditorium. People who had never spoken publicly before were belting out lines and songs. The first play, based on the work ethic in the community, was presented in the elementary school in October 1992 to a packed house. Kimbrel says that the message to the community is that "everybody has a gift to give—you have a gift to give."

From the beginning, the volunteer organizers knew that this could bring the community together in new ways; the experience could cross racial and class boundaries that had never been crossed. Swamp Gravy has done that and more. The plays have strengthened the community more than anyone could have ever known. Volunteers perform, build sets, make costumes, and greet guests in a restored cotton warehouse, contributing thousands of hours of volunteer time to each play. That first play in the elementary school has grown to two plays a year in October and April, played to sellout crowds in a county that has a total population of sixty-five hundred. Thanks to the generosity of a former Colquitt resident, the old cotton warehouse that had stood vacant since the boll weevil brought down King Cotton was transformed into a presentation theater, Cotton Hall.

The Colquitt/Miller Arts Council, the driving force behind Swamp Gravy, has branched out into new areas. The idea of "just a community play" has taken on proportions that Jinks and others could not have imagined more than two decades ago. The council has become a driving economic force in the county, employing sixty people in full-time and part-time jobs at any given period, contributing over $4 million to the local economy in 2005. The Arts Council owns a hotel and restaurant, Tarrer Inn; a skill center, New Life Learning Center, which provides job and life skills as well as traditional craft skills such as quilting and pottery; a multiuse facility for rehearsals, children's programs, and display areas; and Newhall, the home of Swamp Gravy.

Swamp Gravy, as a community play, has a real track record. An original has been written and performed for each of the last twenty years to audiences of almost 150,000 people. It has become an economic force that allows the Arts Council to be a major employer in the county. It has revitalized a small downtown with shops, restaurants, and small businesses. It has created a different legacy and a different future for the community. Swamp Gravy has built a way for people in the community to use arts and culture to build relationships with each other. Many opportunities for expression are part of the community, including the Millennium Mural project begun in 1999 that tells the story of the community visually. Designated as Georgia's first mural city, Colquitt has fifteen murals that celebrate the community's history and culture.

Colquitt will never be the same because of a group of volunteers who had enthusiasm for an idea and worked tirelessly to make it happen, because of the people in the community who shared their lives and histories, and because of hundreds of people who gave up their fears, self-doubts, and time to create something bigger than they ever dreamed. It is a strong case not only for the power of civic leadership but also for the power of inclusiveness.

Even though the play has had dramatic economic effects on the county, there are still large problems looming, such as high rates of teen pregnancies, poverty, and unemployment. With external funding, the Arts Council, the schools, and others are tackling those problems too. The script they see for Colquitt does not begin and end with Swamp Gravy. It includes a community where people feel connected, have access to opportunity, and want to achieve all they can achieve. As the folks there will tell you, this is just the beginning.

In order to realize our assets, we must know who and what are in a community and leverage their collective gifts, talents, and resources for the good of the whole community. The ability to champion our strengths while working diligently on our deficits builds a community's capacity to act on its own behalf. This capacity makes communities work by bringing together human capital, organizational resources, social capital, and outside assistance to galvanize citizens to take responsibility and leverage all their collective resources to improve their community (Chaskin, Brown, Venkatesh, and Vidal, 2001, p. 7).

Asset-based development is common sense. Empowering people to realize the resources and ideas they have to offer is a critical first step for personal and community self-sufficiency.

Chimney Rock, North Carolina: A Mountain and a Plan

When HandMade in America, an economic and community development organization based in Asheville, North Carolina, launched its Small Towns Revitalization Project in 1996, Chimney Rock Village was one of the first towns to participate. The project was directed at towns with populations of less than two thousand people in western North Carolina that were left out of a new craft trails guidebook developed by HandMade; three small towns and a fourth that came in later approached the HandMade staff for help on cataloguing what they had and determining what they needed to do to be part of the heritage tour. As they termed it, they wanted "to put their towns on the craft heritage map." What emerged was a testament to local ingenuity and a laser focus on the assets at hand. Citizens led this effort from the beginning.

The project began with Andrews, Bakersville, Chimney Rock, and Mars Hill. A year later, two more towns joined: Robbinsville and West Jefferson. Six more joined later. The towns were interested for different reasons: some purely economic—getting more tourists in town, some preservation—protecting their culture and heritage from fast-food restaurants, and some community spirit—revitalizing the sense of community. In all places, these priorities were accomplished and much more. The leadership from these small towns realized that inclusion in a guidebook for the thousands of tourists who drive the Blue Ridge Parkway every year was important to their current and future economies. HandMade staff and a resource team from a neighboring town spent two-and-a-half days in each small town, identifying and cataloging its assets—places and things that people who live there every day might miss. Based on the asset catalogue, each town created a strategic plan for the organization, design, marketing, and implementation of their collective vision for their town.

The results of those processes identified for the communities the great assets they had to offer. For example, in Mars Hill the community and the local college had not realized how their interests might mesh. The activities of the college—summer theater, concerts, and the like—had never really been viewed as an asset to the larger community. Another town had a close proximity to a world-famous craft school but had never connected. And finally, Chimney Rock had a beautiful river and river gorge that had been regarded as a liability. Until the 1990s Chimney Rock was a typical mountain tourist town. The shops in town sold lots of T-shirts and rubber snakes. There was little that honored the mountain heritage or the beautiful ecological setting. The Rocky Broad River had always been a bane to their existence: it flooded, there were huge boulders that prevented development, and it hemmed them in. "It was the road, the river, and the rock gorge." One of the reasons that Chimney Rock was so interested in the Small Towns Revitalization Project was because it needed a way to minimize the impact of the river. Six months into the revitalization process, the river reared its angry head and washed away a good portion of the town. As the rebuilding process was under way, the planning group began to think about the river as an asset, not a nuisance. When the number of visitors to Chimney Rock Park increased by 220 percent after it was transformed into an environmental tourist venue, the village of Chimney Rock decided to pursue a nature-based approach in an attempt to entice all the new park visitors into the community. The planning group decided to build their revitalization efforts around ecotourism and actually bring people to the river. The committee used the river boulders to make picnic tables, they cleared brush and made pocket parks, and they created a two-mile creek walk. The change in attitude toward the river ultimately changed the town's retail business: souvenir shops became hiking stores and outdoor clothing shops, and handmade crafts were reintroduced to Main Street. There is now a dress shop and a gem shop, and the town and its merchants are working to keep money flowing into downtown retail. Restaurants built patios overlooking the river and offered picnic baskets for tourists, and business became oriented to the river—now one of Chimney Rock's biggest assets.

Today, Chimney Rock Village is in a different place. The park is now part of the state park system. The village has a partnership with the adjacent town, Lake Lure. Not many communities create a comprehensive plan with a neighboring community, but that is exactly what Chimney Rock and neighboring Lake Lure did in 2013. The partnership with Lake Lure has led to the joint development of walking trails along the river; the adaptation of an abandoned bridge, the Flowering Bridge, as a pedestrian pathway over the river; and the Comprehensive Transportation Plan in the area together. A joint report on their shared "brand" created the "Lofty and Deep" tagline to encompass both communities. According to Chimney Rock Village Mayor Barbara Meliski, "Certainly, this project has shown that both communities have a reinvigorated partnership with each other. We were very pleased with the results, as everyone in both towns had the opportunity to express their opinions, and we look forward to implementing what we have learned" (Town of Lake Lure, 2013). While the two towns want to maintain their individual identities, they believe that their partnership to "brand" the area together can yield positive results for both. Further, there is consistent signage throughout the area, and there is a new charter school, Lake Lure Classical Academy, located near both places. The park hosts a "Music on the Mountain" festival that draws from the region; the village offers music and nightlife, and there are more shops downtown—developments that were almost unthinkable when they started the revitalization process.

Chimney Rock is a small town and is likely to stay one, but it has lots of staying power and is full of assets. As the director of Chimney Rock Park, Mary Jaeger Gale, puts it, "We are a leader-full community."

Assets Disguised as Liabilities

Texas always seems to do things bigger and a little different. In the case of two small towns, they are doing things smarter. Community members too often ignore obvious circumstances or conditions that could provide new opportunities and uses. While some things may seem obvious on first glance, such as an historic building or neighborhood, some are under the radar.

It is no secret that the country's population is becoming more urban. Less than 20 percent of us live outside metropolitan areas. Small towns have been inversely affected by this trend. In addition to the demographic shift to larger cities, smaller communities have seen traditional businesses lost to big-box store competition and once-traveled rural highways replaced with the circumvention of the interstate highway system. One town in Texas, Saluda, epitomized the storm of circumstances that can devastate small towns. Located in central Texas, the town was once home to a college, mills, and very handsome housing stock that the owners and overseers built at the turn of the twentieth century. After the college burned down, the mills flooded, and the wealthier class moved away, the last straw for the town was the building of Interstate 35 about a mile from the town center. Those who had traveled through Saluda on their way to the state capital in Austin or Fort Hood could bypass Saluda altogether. But the Saludians had a different idea. Knowing that destination weddings were becoming popular, locals bought and refurbished a number of the antebellum homes to create a cluster of places for wedding sites and getaway weekends ("Reviving Small Towns . . . ," 2006). The shift has worked. It is hard to get a reservation now in Saluda. Farther down the state in the Rio Grande Valley, Hidalgo had a problem more deadly than merely a faltering economy: the town had killer bees. Planted squarely in the migration pattern of the African killer bees, Hidalgo dreaded the bee season beginning about 1950. But twenty years ago, the town had another idea: embrace the problem as an opportunity. After erecting a twenty-foot Killer Bee statue, the community dubbed itself the "Killer Bee Capital of the World" and embraced the bee as a tourism draw. The town has a minor league hockey team call the Rio Grande Valley Killer Bees, sells T-shirts and souvenirs that feature the bee, and respects the bee for what it can inflict but also for what it is doing for Hidalgo ("Reviving Small Towns . . . ," 2006).

Connect Clusters of Assets to Build Synergy

Being strategic as well as nostalgic is not a bad thing. Community members who remember the downtown Strand Theatre or the historic post office or train station can take comfort that if they are interested in how it was, others might be also. Far too often we cannot imagine how a building, a street, or a cultural icon would look if it were vibrant again.

Rural and urban economies are beginning to reclaim their natural environment and cultural past as key economic resources. Amenities such as rivers, mountains, trails, and so on are now being correlated with job growth and population enhancements (Hibbard, Lurie, and Morrison, 2012). We are learning more and more about the synergistic relationship that is built when amenities are connected. The idea of "clustering" put forth by Michael Porter (2000) goes far beyond similar or complementary businesses to a defining idea for places that want to highlight their collective assets. A plethora of "roads," "trails," and "districts" have packaged themselves together to garner more visitors, more dollars, and more visibility. There are the Mississippi Blues Trail, the Lake County California Quilt Trail, and the Maine Art Museum Trail, for example. These kinds of loose collaborations generate a range of investments, attractions, job opportunities, and financial rewards. Rarely does the designation of one area jumpstart the whole economy. The "tipping point" occurs when a cluster of companies, arts venues, restaurants, historical sites, and recreational opportunities reinforce and build on each other (Gladwell, 2000).

Decisions must be made collectively about the value added of potential community assets; the process is clearly goal directed— improving the economic vitality of the area or saving a valued community icon. There are always subgoals such as civic pride and social capital, but the primary focus is usually repositioning a community to be more competitive.

An added dimension to the theory and practice of cumulative capital is the evolving interest in creative placemaking (Markusen and Gadwa, 2010) and the attention given to involving citizens in the design and adaptation of communities. Placemaking underscores the ability to design a more robust quality of life that is inclusive and sustainable and that is connected. Creative placemaking is not about one organization or institution in a community or even several; it is about the interconnection of arts and culture with the life of the city. The interspersion of artists and creators within a place creates a synergy of activities and initiatives. Small towns in particular can benefit from building on a distinctive cultural and artistic niche. HandMade in America connected venues around the region through its craft trails so that tourists and others were drawn to the whole, not just the parts. The HandMade "map" was drawn not only in the largest population area of Asheville, but also in the towns and hamlets throughout western North Carolina. This early example of placemaking has had a huge impact on the region with its promotion of the "invisible factory" of artisans and craftspeople.

Linking parts to create a great whole is exactly the strategy used to connect a whole series of music venues into the euphemistic "Crooked Road" in southwest Virginia that stretches three hundred miles east/west from Galax to Clintwood. Along the miles of road are the Floyd General Store, whose front porch is filled on Friday nights with fiddle players, banjo pickers, and harmonizers from the local area, to Galax and its Blue Ridge Music Center and Barr's Fiddle Shop, to The Ralph Stanley Museum and Traditional Mountain Music Center in Clintwood, Virginia. All along the trail, southwest Virginia's rich music heritage is on display. Spurred by interest from ten counties, three cities, ten towns, five regional planning districts, and four state agencies, the "Road" has generated a new stream of revenue for the venues and the affiliated partners of restaurants, other attractions, and motels and hotels. The "Road" connects sights, people, and places that have been there all along in new ways. While it seems strange to say that a "cluster" extends three hundred miles and includes interstates, four-lane highways, and switchback mountain roads—in fact, that is exactly what it does. Being able to provide high-quality music, arts venues, or historical sites in multiples of more than one is a critical first step in an economic development strategy.

Building on the historical assets of areas continues to be a viable option for community and economic developers. For the past twenty years, Portland, Maine, has boomed as a charming tourist destination that also draws professionals and retirees looking for a vibrant, livable community with an authentic New England atmosphere and unique arts culture.

Portland's success has depended on its ability to negotiate the transition between an industrial economy based on shipbuilding and fishing to a commercial economy that maintains a connection to its historic maritime identity. Unlike many industrial cities that floundered in the mid- to late twentieth century, Portland found an opportunity to restructure its economy by building on an invaluable asset: its maritime history and culture. In 1987 the City of Portland passed legislation to prevent nonmarine development on its waterfront to protect maritime businesses and then worked cooperatively and creatively with both developers and the fishing industry to ensure the economic and historic vitality of the Old Port. One successful example of this is the recent renovation by the Pierce Atwood law firm of the Cumberland Cold Storage building on Commercial Street.

The Cumberland Cold Storage building, built between 1884 and 1924 as a spice mill and canning plant, has been a fixture on Merrill Wharf for decades. Although of modest architectural significance, it serves an important place in the fabric of the waterfront's character. When Pierce Atwood, a large Portland law firm, was looking to change its headquarters, it saw the Cumberland Cold Storage building as a prime location; however, there were several hurdles that had to be overcome to make this viable.

Correspondingly, the city saw the benefits of having a large, prosperous law firm with approximately two hundred employees working and living in the downtown area and also having a significant building along the waterfront renovated, so they decided to work with the firm to enable the restoration while maintaining their dedication to the fishermen on the wharf.

Leveraging existing assets for economically viable reuse can be an arduous process. If it were simply an inventory or a replication of best practices, all communities would have a full slate. Experience teaches us that identifying and then leveraging assets is not a general application of a set of guidelines, but requires a careful analysis of the space, place, and culture that is particular to each locale. HandMade in America identified eight factors as critical to successful renewal (Hunter and McGill, 1999):

1. Self-help and accountability—helping communities help themselves
2. Citizen leadership
3. Building on the heritage, resources, desires, hopes, and aspirations of the community
4. Involvement of the whole community
5. Incremental learning
6. Going at the pace of the community
7. Sharing stories to help citizens begin to hear and talk to one another
8. Creating new and enduring partnerships

Community members, policymakers, and local leadership must be intentional, think in new ways, and be willing to undertake risk as they approach asset-based community development. Nobel Laureate Douglas North (2005) coined the concept of "adaptive efficiency" to argue how economic change occurs. He defined it by saying that it is the "willingness of society to acquire knowledge and learning, to induce innovation, to undertake risk and creative activity of all sorts, as well as resolve problems and bottlenecks of the society through time." North identifies intentionality as a crucial variable in social learning. Whether under economic siege or not, the goal for communities is to enhance their quality of life and economic vitality to ensure that they are competitive as place becomes a major consideration of business and population location. Building on existing assets is critical to positive change and long-term resilience and must be intentional.

The asset-based approach does not sugarcoat the negatives, but rather places communities in a position to uncover resources that were either unused or ill used. Kretzmann and McKnight (1993) conclude their book, *Building Communities from the Inside Out*, with two pieces of advice: first, although outside resources are still very much needed in low-income communities, their impact will be wasted if the inside community capacity is not developed or awakened; and second, outside resources that dominate or control a community's efforts and potential will weaken the ability of the community to leverage the resources. The community must maintain a level of independence and a vision of itself.

So how to decide what is an asset to be kept and leveraged? Asset-based approaches do not take the place of smart public policy. They cannot make up for years of disinvestment, isolation, or lack of jobs, but they can make it possible for interventions to work when they might not otherwise. This approach can position a community and its investors to think and see differently. The cataloguing of assets is a process that leads to a product: a renewed sense of community tangibles, a start toward new relationships, and an approach that begins where people live.

CHAPTER FIVE

Practicing Democracy

In 2013 in Warrenton, Virginia, a small town near Washington, D.C., the town's two-hundred-year-old newspaper, *The Fauquier Times-Democrat*, decided to drop "Democrat" from its name because of the partisanship climate that exists most everywhere these days. The paper said it was a business decision to appeal to new people in the community.

This is a small example of a country in a crisis of consensus. Over the last several decades, we have seen an erosion of our ability to talk and reason with each other over issues that are critical to our collective long-term prosperity. There have always been partisanship, labels, and divisiveness, but the latest incarnation has led to a civic paralysis that stymies the ability to act and the critical democratic skill of deliberation. The public has drawn the line in the sand on political, social, and religious issues, and our politicians lack the ability to debate and decide, a process critical to a healthy society. The government shutdown in 2013 was division at its worst. As policies and politics are shaped more by special interests, the role and the voice of citizens have become endangered in some communities. But there is good news. Communities throughout the United States are engaging citizens every day in discussions, deliberations, and decisions on the best course of action for their collective future. And it is working. Civic engagement has become a catchphrase for almost everything that occurs outside the private realm, but even in its most general application it carries three important assumptions. First, people can have a voice and make a difference. Second, solutions require new approaches; and third, new solutions can only come through the collective voice. Communities that respond effectively to the problems, challenges, and opportunities which come their way understand the need for the active participation of a broad range and large number of ordinary citizens, not just those with formal decision-making authority.

As McCoy and Scully (2002) write, most people don't choose a door marked "engagement" or "civic," but rather begin the process by getting involved in an issue they care about. It might be something very close to home, like the fate of a neighborhood park, or it might be global, such as the preservation of the Amazon rain forest, but it drives their passion and concern. As this work continues, it is not done in isolation: engagement is done with other people.

Deliberation between and among people in a community helps solve problems—clearly and simply. Those places that have embedded talking together into their *modus operandi* are stronger economically, and they have larger stores of social capital. The dialogue provides an outlet for new ideas and more civic involvement, and creates the pathway to active problem solving. The community examples highlighted here all speak to the importance of the deliberative process to a strong democracy. Each in its own way illustrates that every community can have a new way to discuss and decide together on the strategies to address the critical issues of the day.

In this era of information deluge—push notifications, tweeting, and news updates—it may be hard to believe that people don't have enough information to make knowledgeable decisions. But too often issues are presented as "snapshots," not as the whole portfolio. This lack of knowledge on issues provides an opportunity for nonprofit organizations, community groups, and local governments to join with the public to learn more about the challenges the community is facing and to provide forums in which people can address them. This is exactly the mission of the three approaches profiled in this chapter: the Oregon Citizens' Initiative Review, Jacksonville Community Council, Inc., and the Hampton Civic Engagement initiatives.

A Different Kind of Politics

There are two kinds of politics at play in communities, according to Mathews (1999). The first is centered on the election cycle and is found in political campaigns, voting, and political speeches. The second, which must go on regardless of elections, is based on the working of communities and is found in "neighborhood associations, public forums, and organizations for civic action" (p. 122). Both are necessary for a healthy democracy; however, it is the second form of politics that informs the first.

Democracy becomes real for people when they move beyond the political candidate or campaign they support and decide what kind of community they want. The core of our democracy is the opportunity to discuss, deliberate, and decide what is in the public or community's interest, irrespective of divisive partisanship. This is known as *deliberative democracy.*

Deliberative democracy is not a one-way street or a collection of talking heads. Rather, it is an approach to politics that includes citizens, experts, and politicians in solving problems and making decisions. There are four core principles that drive this form of community problem solving according to Carcasson and Sprain (2010):

1. *Tough choices.* In a diverse and globalized system of democracy, there are not only competing opinions but also competing values. Our system has encouraged us to be adversarial and stand our ground. Deliberation encourages new ways to frame and discuss issues that can help citizens work through difficult issues and propose possible solutions that can be implemented.

2. *Public judgment.* This is the ability to collectively work through the uncertainty that exists around all public issues. As Barber (1988) writes, "The journey from private opinion to political judgment does not follow a road from prejudice to true knowledge; it proceeds from solitude to sociability." Of course, some things have no clear-cut answers; there are complex and competing interests. But unless the goal is inaction, we must talk, learn, and then decide.

3. *Democratic governance.* This presumes that these tough problems need engagement and participation from the whole community. "Broad collaborative efforts," write Carcasson and Sprain (2010), "that move away from a focus on government as sole problem solver can work to

transcend political partisanship, empower local communities, and lead to systemic changes that go beyond an ongoing focus on addressing symptoms."

4. *Inclusiveness and equality.* For deliberative dialogue and resulting actions to have legitimacy, agency, and sustainability, these efforts must be inclusive and representative of the community. This is not easy work. It requires knowing the whole community and inviting them into the larger conversation. The old model of "representatives" of one group or another doesn't work anymore. Rarely, if ever, can one person or one small group speak on behalf of gender, race, socioeconomic status, special interests, and so forth, in an effective way.

Community dialogue needs a big tent. These principles of deliberative democracy provide guidance for communities to find better ways to build their economy and their quality of life. The civic goal, then, is to identify vehicles that allow for dialogue and deliberation that lead to action.

Recognizing That a Problem Is a Problem

The first step toward a deliberative democracy is widespread community engagement, and there are two main barriers to broad-based civic involvement that any community must work to overcome.

First, many citizens are unaware of the nature and seriousness of problems in their communities. If citizens do not believe certain problems are issues in their own community, they cannot work to address them. Political scientists have found that while people tend to praise their elected representative in Congress or the local school system, they often distrust or criticize the institution of Congress or public education generally. Perhaps the same dynamic is at work here: people recognize such problems as hunger, housing, and the quality of public education as national issues but often do not see the manifestations of these problems in their home community.

So how do you get citizens to realize an issue affects them? Luke (1998) identifies four elements that must be in place for issues to gain prominence in the public's concern. First, there must be a rise in awareness. Take for example, the response by the public to the information about child safety seats. In 1965 a group called the Physicians for Automotive Safety picketed the New York Automobile Show about the dangers to children unrestrained in vehicles. In 1971 the group published a pamphlet directed at parents about the risks, and the National Transportation Safety Board established the first federal standards, but with no accompanying crash tests. A year later *Consumer Reports* said that most of the cars on the road would not pass the crash test. Six full years later, in 1978, Tennessee was the first state to pass child safety seat legislation. Today all fifty states, the District of Columbia, Guam, the Northern Mariana Islands, and the Virgin Islands require child safety seats for infants and children fitting specified criteria. It took time and information.

Second, there must be emotional ties and an urgency to the issue. While we have seen citizens become involved in an issue as "just the right thing to do," more often it is because of a personal attachment, observed experience, or an emotional connection for some reason. Media and marketing companies often use children and animals to sell products. Why? It tugs at people's emotions. The same is true with systemic community issues. National statistics about homelessness create a vague picture in people's minds of what it is like to be on the street. Meeting a homeless family or hearing about a child's experiences changing schools multiple times during the school year gives a context and impetus for action.

The public must believe that the problem is urgent. This is probably the most difficult step. Being able to convey the "opportunity costs and benefits" of acting immediately is a critical stage in problem solving. Take educational achievement, for example. Research has shown that if students are not reading at grade level by the fourth grade, in all likelihood they will never recover. Rationally, we know that reading is cumulative and that students get better over time. It is impossible to catch up over night. However, it is often difficult to get community support to intervene early and to see the connection between reading skills and later workforce preparation. Do we think they will magically catch up during the summer between third and fourth grade?

Communicating why certain investments are time sensitive is a critical part of the larger deliberative process.

Finally, there must be a belief that the problem can be addressed successfully. If citizens believe that the barriers are too high and the problems too bad, they feel they cannot do anything. It is important that people understand where to begin, what can get done, and how the pieces fit together. To do that, they need to talk about it.

Once residents are aware of the nature and seriousness of their community's problems, they must have the ability to work through them in a deliberative and democratic way. Yankelovich finds that it is more than just information that is needed; it is the ability to think through and then act on an issue in a reasonable way. "To be excited about an issue and then fail to think it through makes for the worst kind of citizen" (1988, p. 33).

A Public Willing to Act

In order to understand the potential impact of the deliberative process, it is important to know the public's willingness to act on new information and new perspectives. A barrier to participation for many people is that they are unsure of whom to contact or how to get involved in their communities.

A survey commissioned by the Pew Partnership for Civic Change in 2003, *What Will It Take? Making Headway on Our Most Wrenching Problems,* shows that America is brimming with individuals who are ready and willing to get involved in improving the quality of life in their communities. The survey results depict the public as a resource whose collective skills and enthusiasm could be brought together to address a range of persistent problems.

A 2013 report from the Pew Research Center on Civic Engagement in the Digital Age had similar findings. A large number of Americans, nearly 50 percent, said that they had directly taken part in a civic group or activity during the last twelve months. One-third of those worked with others to solve a problem.

One of the emerging trends in the engagement arena is the variety of technological tools—social networking, online petitions, viral videos, and so on—that can be used to engage the willing public in political and bureaucratic processes. The 2013

Pew report found that social networking is not a separate realm of political activity, but just one of many ways that people engage with the issues. Every day, new opportunities for technological engagement in democracy are emerging that extend beyond social networking to more tangible and meaningful deliberative politics and engagement.

The Changing Shape of Engagement

In June of 2013, the John S. and James L. McKnight Foundation and MIT's Center for Civic Media hosted a conference on the changing shape of civic engagement. It was entitled "Insiders and Outsiders." For the event, leading media innovators were invited to discuss the potential of public participation in political processes within a world of increased digital technology and literacy (Whitacre, 2013).

Several questions were asked of participants, including the following: How can a new set of tactics such as online petitions, viral videos, civic crowdfunding, and collective brainstorming complement traditional modes of community engagement? How can we use technology to stretch the potential of public participation to make it more engaging, responsive, creative, constructive, and open to all citizens? What does it mean to be inside and outside of government, and what does it mean to make new civic spaces in government? What is "open government"? (Whitacre, 2013).

All of these questions center on the position of the digital citizen, the role of the government in a more digital world, and the potential of technology for civic engagement. In a day of blurry roles, ever-expanding possibilities because of technological advances, and an increasingly tech-savvy citizenry, they could not come at a better time.

The Digital Citizen

Digital citizenship is defined as the "ability to participate in society online," and digital citizens are those who use prevailing forms of communication regularly and effectively (Mossberger, Tolbert, and McNeal, 2008). Since the advent of online social networking and social media, digital citizens have been able to participate in the civic process *politically* and technologically. That is, they can start online petitions and viral videos and work individually or collaborate to support certain candidates or reform specific laws or rebuke judicial decisions. They can post opinions publicly and have immediate responses, comments, and discussions with others.

While political engagement has an important place within our democratic society, this kind of participation does not require citizens to work hand-in-hand with the actual government entity or vice versa. Only in recent years have local and state governments begun to use the concept of digital citizenship to engage residents in government *bureaucracy*—that is, the everyday workings and responsibilities of the government offices.

This new type of civic engagement is important for several reasons. Primarily, it requires the government to be open and responsive to the needs of the digital citizen and more transparent in its processes. Second, it inspires a more dynamic relationship between a citizen and his or her government. For example, if a local city improves its services, what can it ask in return for these new and improved services?

In her TED Talk, Jennifer Pahlka, founder of Code for America, argues that one issue with our current framework for civic engagement is that we think our input to the government system is voting, not participation between election cycles in the less sexy forms of bureaucracy. However, she gives examples of how the digital citizen can help government systems and services—making them more efficient, effective, and streamlined—in the physical world (Pahlka, 2012).

Every town in America has a call center used for issues ranging from fires to downed trees in roads to opossums in garbage cans. Citizens can call, and a representative from the appropriate local municipal department will be sent to fix the problem. However, in many cases these issues could be fixed simply and more cheaply just with the help of a neighbor.

Citizens Connect, a web and mobile app developed by the Office of New Urban Mechanics in Boston, is a platform for connection with citizens to alleviate just these types of problems. Recently, there was a post on the website that said:

Possum in my trash can. Can't tell if it's dead . . . How do I get this removed? (Pahlka, 2012)

A few hours later, there was another post from a neighbor:

Walked over to West Ninth Street . . . Locate trash behind house. Possum? Check. Living? Yep. Turned the trash can on its side. Walked home. Good night, sweet possum. (Pahlka, 2012)

At first glance, this might seem like a simple and somewhat humorous example; however, it exemplifies how digital citizenry can change the role of government and how citizens can participate in community work. In this example, the government was not playing one of its traditional roles—that is, municipal fire, water, or garbage service—but was acting as a connecting platform for citizens to engage with one another. The Citizens Connect service allowed a solution to be reached quickly, effectively, and much more cheaply than if a staff member had to be called to go to the resident's house and solve the problem—saving staff time and taxpayers' dollars and allowing municipal employees to focus on more critical issues.

Open Government

The idea of *open government* is a theory intrinsically linked to the potential of the digital citizen to engage meaningfully with government. In the past thirty years or so, the term *open government* has been associated with transparency and accountability in government affairs and decision-making processes. Within the past decade, it has become such a hot political issue that President Barack Obama issued a memorandum entitled "Transparency and Open Government" on his first day of office in 2009. Most important, his memorandum makes two points: 1) information maintained by the government is a public asset; and 2) it should be disclosed in forms that the public can "readily find and use" (Obama, 2009).

In relation to digital citizenship, open government becomes tied directly to the public's access to government data. In these days, open government cannot exist without open data. Open data can make government transparency easier, bridging the gap between government policies and their effects on individuals' everyday lives, and be the basis of a deliberative dialogue.

Often municipal and state governments are not equipped to make good decisions or innovations on technology—by the time an idea (like Boston's Citizens Connect app) can jump through the bureaucratic red tape needed to get funded, it might already be out of date—however, they are in a position to make data available. Then the cities can work with private developers or volunteers or host events such as civic hackathons to create apps, portals, or games that help citizens utilize the data. In this way, the government can let the innovators do what they do best, and it can facilitate the process with open, up-to-date data.

Several cities have taken advantage of this strategy to their benefit. On June 1, 2013, more than ninety cities across the nation took part in a National Day of Civic Hacking with the purpose being to "collaboratively create, build, and invent new solutions using publicly released data, code, and technology to solve challenges relevant to our neighborhoods, our cities, our states, and our country" (Hack for Change, 2013). The civic hackers were ordinary community members and volunteers; however, with this event they were able to meaningfully participate in their local government and use their technical skills for positive (and quick) change.

For example, a group from Minneapolis was frustrated with not knowing the public bus system's schedules and route times. So in conjunction with the Chief Information Office of Minneapolis, the hackers worked to create a website that displays nearby bus times and distances, provides information on arriving bus routes, and maps bus stops near a user. This web portal will work to make public transportation easier and more efficient for the Minneapolis citizen. And now the team is working on a mobile app version that can integrate with Minneapolis's Metro transit website (Brennan, 2013).

Another team from Kansas City was disturbed when the historic Orion Building was torn down in April 2013. Guided by a mission for historic preservation, it used that city's hackathon to create a new website called Teardown Tattler, which monitors city data and public records, tracking building demolition permits, and makes the material available publicly. Concerned residents can use that information to see endangered buildings and their addresses and take action to save historic properties and the Kansas City skyline before they are demolished (Brennan, 2013).

Last, a group from Oakland, California, was fed up with the difficulty of finding information and services on city government websites. They realized that most people turn to a search engine, usually Google or Bing, to begin their Internet journeys. They thought that this framework could be an intuitive way for citizens to receive simple, easy-to-understand responses on city services. On Oakland Answers, citizens can type questions regarding such topics as "How do I get a permit for constructing a building?" into a simple search box and receive an answer telling them where to apply and "What you need to know" in order to do so.

Several interesting insights on civic engagement can be gleaned from the projects resulting from the National Day of Civic Hacking. First, these projects enable citizens to engage around topics that are important and meaningful to them—whether that is saving historic structures or being able to get to and from home more efficiently. Second, citizens can collaborate to solve problems quickly and efficiently. Third, through working with city officials and data, citizens can have more empathy and understanding for the work that municipal offices do. Last, citizens can help to make government services more efficient, not just weigh in on government decisions.

Programs such as the National Day of Civic Hacking are changing the ways in which citizens can engage meaningfully with various levels of government and also each other. While these changes have almost unlimited potential and possibility, several limitations or challenges still must be addressed. The speakers on the "Opening Open Government" panel at the civic media conference mentioned previously outlined a few of these challenges:

1. *Keeping the humans in the system:* It is important to make sure that the technological innovations (apps, portals, and so on) do not become more important than the people who will need to use them.

2. *Efficiency versus transparency:* Often creating more government transparency through the release of public data does not make government processes and decisions more

efficient. A balance or medium must be found between efficiency and transparency.

3. *Funding:* The issues that organizations or donors want to fund do not necessarily correspond with the needs of the city, such as garbage collection.

4. *Technological limitations:* Even when government employees and offices want to provide the data, the technology itself can be a barrier to releasing it in a way that can be consumed by citizens.

5. *Culture of inertia:* Governments are used to moving slowly and being hesitant to release data, even if it is publicly owned.

6. *Lack of incentives:* There has to be an incentive on both sides—the citizen and the government—for change to take place. (Whitacre, 2013)

These challenges suggest that there is room for growth in understanding the role of the engaged digital citizen and the relationship between the digital citizen and his or her government. Beyond just the technology and the available data, the strength of our democracy depends on our ability to discuss, decide, and do together. The examples profiled take different approaches to making the process of change possible.

Oregon Citizens' Initiative Review: More Informed Voters

The Oregon Citizens' Initiative Review (CIR) is a program developed by Healthy Democracy Oregon with the goal of providing Oregon voters with clear, useful, and trustworthy information on statewide ballot measures. It was adopted into Oregon law in 2011, following a 2010 pilot process, and is the first program of its kind to be approved by any state in the United States.

The program is beneficial and helps support the democratic process in Oregon in two ways. First, it provides unbiased evaluations and information on statewide measures, helping voters make more informed decisions on their ballots. A study conducted by the Kettering Foundation and The Pennsylvania State University found that 2/3 of statement readers in 2012 found the panelists' insights helpful in making their own voting decisions (Knobloch, Gastil, Richards, and Feller, 2013). "Those who read the CIR statements learned more about the ballot measures than those who read other portions of the official Voters Guide" (Gastil, 2012). Second, the CIR engages citizens from all demographic and geographic areas in the state's electoral process, encouraging a culture of informed democracy. In 2012, 51 percent of Oregon voters were aware of the CIR by the conclusion of the election cycle (Knobloch et al., 2013).

So what is the Oregon CIR and how does it work? For each measure on the state ballot, twenty-four randomly selected panel members from all regions of the state are brought together for five days of critical evaluation and deliberation on the issue at hand. The composition of the panel corresponds with the gender, age, ethnicity, location, and party affiliation of the state electorate. Over the course of the five days, the panel hears arguments for and against the measure by advocates, policy experts, and witnesses. They are given the opportunity to ask questions, prioritize issues, and deliberate together.

Throughout every step of the process, critical measures are taken to ensure fairness and neutrality in the proceedings. For example, supporters of each side are given equal time allotments to make their cases, and professional, unbiased mediators facilitate the deliberations.

At the conclusion of the five-day session, the panel drafts a "Citizens' Statement" highlighting the most important findings about the measure, including significant arguments and how many panelists support or oppose it. This statement is then published as part of the Voters' Pamphlet mailed to every voter in the state to use during election time.

Jacksonville Community Council, Inc.: Deciding the Future

Another group that found its calling in engaging ordinary citizens in the betterment of their community is the Jacksonville Community Council, Inc. During the 1960s, the city of Jacksonville, Florida, was poised to enter a period of tremendous physical growth and development. Community leaders and elected officials began to realize that a number of serious problems facing the city could only be addressed effectively with widespread support from the community.

In 1974 the president-elect of the Jacksonville Area Chamber of Commerce convened a three-day planning meeting for one hundred civic leaders from the city and Duval County, including public officials, city council members, labor representatives, military personnel, religious leaders, and business executives. At a pivotal time in Jacksonville's history, representatives from a fragmented community with diverse sectional interests came together and talked about Jacksonville, its problems, and its opportunities. The participants created a priority list of critical issues facing the community and developed a shared commitment to solve the identified problems. Further, the participants agreed that there needed to be a mechanism for continuing the dialogue begun at the conference. The result was the decision to establish the Jacksonville Community Council, Inc. (JCCI), a nonprofit, broad-based civic organization that began operation in 1975.

JCCI "makes things happen" by organizing and administering two continuing activities that play a key role in improving life in the Jacksonville area. One is the annual publication of Quality of Life Indicators—reports that assess the state of the economy, education, the environment, public safety, health, and other matters vital to the quality of life for Jacksonville area residents. The second activity is the formation and guidance of annual citizen-based study committees charged with responsibility for fully, fairly, and accurately exploring an important issue of community concern. The task for each committee is to analyze the issue carefully, to ascertain the facts involved, and to ensure that it is examined from multiple points of view.

The study committee process begins in the spring. The JCCI board identifies the problems or issues for study. The president of the board then selects a volunteer to chair the study committee meetings. In turn, the chair chooses the members of a volunteer management team to help shepherd the process. Over the summer, JCCI staff perform background research on the problem or issue and work with the chair and management team to develop a calendar of weekly meetings.

In September, through its newsletter, press releases, and public service announcements, JCCI solicits volunteers from the community to serve on the committees. Sixty to one hundred people typically sign up to participate in a study committee. During the next year, committee members study, discuss, and ultimately decide on recommendations to go forward. The process is time intensive and thorough. As generally understood, consensus means that all who have participated in a group's discussions can live with—or go along with—the conclusions the group reaches. It does not mean complete agreement, nor does it mean that participants are equally satisfied with—or enthusiastic about—the result. But it does mean that they recognize that the result is the best one for the community as a whole and the best that practically can be achieved.

After four decades of JCCI's existence, a distinctive model of citizen-based, consensus decision making has emerged. Among other things, the model is unique in its successful blending of citizen-based consensual decision making with the technical, financial, and logistical strengths of organizational human services planning. Since 1977 more than eighty citizen studies have been conducted with a high number of recommendations being implemented. For example, in response to a study on teen pregnancy, an innovative youth center, the Bridge of Northeast Florida, was established to assist young people in making better life choices. JCCI estimates that the recommendations contained in study committee reports are fully or partially implemented between 80 and 85 percent of the time. Even more important, JCCI's efforts have fostered the growth of a civic culture in Jacksonville in which citizens now expect that they will participate in, contribute to, and exercise tangible influence over any key decision made by municipal government.

As a result of being made a full partner in governing their community, citizens have been willing to take greater responsibility for solving the problems and addressing the issues confronting Jacksonville. In 2000, for example, voters approved overwhelmingly an increase in the sales tax to generate revenue for downtown capital improvements. JCCI's efforts have helped residents of the Jacksonville area to understand, appreciate, and embrace citizen-driven, consensus-based decision making. JCCI sustains citizen interest through continual citizen participation in identifying the problems or issues to be studied, obtaining and analyzing data concerning them, and refining indicators that illuminate the quality of life that currently prevails in the community.

JCCI's latest effort is JAX2025 launched in 2012. A large-scale effort, with an array of partners, the goal is to come to agreement as a community on what the core functions of government should be and also on the long-term vision for the community and its priorities. According to Ben Warner, executive director of JCCI, "There was not an explicit goal for the city that everyone could get behind."

Since September of 2012, more than sixteen thousand people have participated in the JAX2025 process by attending a forum, completing a questionnaire, or attending community follow-up meetings. Respondents to the community survey represented 183 ZIP Codes with none having more than 5 percent of the total responses. During the process, participants have come from all parts of the community. The responses yielded ten target visions of where they want the community to be excelling in 2025: education, economy, distinctive neighborhoods, a vibrant downtown with arts and entertainment, a diverse inclusive community, a place where people matter, a clean and green city, exemplary governance, transportation, and a health community. In June of 2013, four task forces were announced to begin the action portion of JAX2025. These task forces will address Distinctive Neighborhoods, Working Together for People, Government Openness and Responsiveness, and Encouraging Bicycle and Pedestrian Transportation. In addition, organizations, government, and individuals are working through sixty organizational items identified by the survey and addressing each with one of three strategies:

- They Should (what community organizations should be doing)
- You Can (what individuals can do to help)
- I Will (personal commitment to act)

There has been enormous support from media, government, funders, and literally thousands of people for the communitywide effort. Where will Jacksonville and Duval County be in 2025? Where they want to be.

Hampton: Local Government as Convenor and Listener

The citizens of Hampton, Virginia, have been, for almost twenty years, the beneficiary—and partner—of a city government that both grasps and puts into practice the basic truth that democratic government must not be just for the people, but of them and by them as well.

In 1987 the City of Hampton's proposed General Plan Update (of its 1977 plan) provoked intense opposition from neighborhood groups in the northern part of the city. Citizens were irate because the update included a plan to build a new east-west freeway to relieve traffic on a major thoroughfare. The projected increases in traffic volume pointed to a severe traffic crisis within the next ten to fifteen years. An even more important reason for the anger of neighborhood associations in the area was that they had not been consulted about how to deal with the traffic problem, and in particular, about the proposed freeway solution. In many respects, Hampton's experience in 1987 was typical of the way many municipal governments in American cities have tried to solve problems historically. The usual procedure has been for city planners to analyze the problem, develop options, choose the best solution from among them, and present it to the city council for approval. Sometimes public hearings are held to receive citizen comments on the proposed solution. But seldom does such input have a substantial impact on the plan that has already been developed. Hampton's response was anything but typical. The city manager at the time held a meeting with the neighborhood groups and proposed that they join city government in a consensus-based process to produce a new plan that would generate a solution acceptable to everyone. The neighborhood associations agreed. City staff and representatives of the neighborhood associations developed a list of stakeholders and formed an initiating committee, consisting of representatives from four neighborhood groups, three business groups, and three members of city staff. The assistant city manager was selected to serve as facilitator. The committee met weekly for four months, during which time they set the ground rules for the consensus process. After agreeing on the rules and participants in the process, the committee took its proposal to a large group of stakeholders, who approved it at a public meeting. Finally, a working committee was assembled, comprising the members of the initiating committee, the chair of the planning commission, a representative of the affected business interests, and two at-large citizens from other areas of the city.

Beginning in late 1988, the working committee held a three-hour meeting every week or two. All meetings were open and were well covered by a local newspaper. When ideas or suggestions were made, neighborhood groups and others were invited to attend the meetings of the committee. After a year, the working committee produced a plan that most people agreed was not only acceptable, but actually better than the one proposed originally by the city. Just a few years later, the city took the initiative to apply its collaborative model to the topic of public education. The question quickly became one of healthy youth development more generally. The result was the establishment of a youth coalition and a strategic plan for youth development. The success of the 1987 General Plan Update and the subsequent youth development initiative set off a wave of changes during the 1990s in the way the City of Hampton works, and in the way it relates to the community it serves today. According to Terry O'Neill, director of community development, "Engagement is built into the culture of the community. It is what community members want and expect. The community has come to expect to be engaged in decision making. It is business as usual." Just a few of the results from the early process include the following:

- The Neighborhood Commission has been created, which is composed of representatives of neighborhoods from ten districts.

- Neighborhood grants programs to foster neighborhood improvement and communication have been developed.

- City government as a whole—not just the Planning Department—has adopted collaborative decision making as a way of doing business. There is now a deeply rooted culture of collaboration within city government.

- Citizens have a positive view of city government and the way it conducts its business. Distrust of the city has greatly diminished. Citizens feel empowered. If they don't like something, they express it.

- A large and growing number of citizens have participated in consensus-based interactions with city staff. Many have taken advantage of opportunities the city provides (including the Neighborhood College and Hampton & You) to increase their knowledge of city government, to develop their own collaborative skills, and to build expertise in areas ranging from parenting to résumé writing. These efforts have increased Hampton's pool of community leaders. Over the past twenty years, several citizens have received the inspiration and acquired the skills needed in order to run for and be elected to city council.

- The city's Youth Commission is nationally known for involving young people in substantive decision making.

More generally, the city's commitment to involving as many citizens as possible in collaborative decision making has helped build a stronger sense of community. According to O'Neill, the community is always trying to make the tried-and-true forms of engagement more effective but also testing out new tools to make conversations and interactions more convenient.

A community spirit has emerged that has enabled and encouraged citizens to feel real ownership of their neighborhoods, their community, and their city government. When the community has gone through tough budget years, civic engagement and youth programming have scored high on those things to continue. Along with this sense of ownership has come an acceptance by citizens of responsibility for helping solve the problems and meet the challenges their neighborhoods and community face. Citizens in Hampton today are much less disposed than previously to ask what city government can do for them. Instead they ask how they can work with government to get things done.

Can We Talk?

Communities often have no place, space, or convener that allows for citizens to come together and deliberate. The avenues for participation usually are found in formal public meetings, fiery special-interest sessions, or the morning breakfast group conversation at the local diner. These all have their place, but there must be vehicles for regular, ongoing dialogue that has currency with people. We need opportunities that allow citizens to do more than just talk, but rather talk, decide, and do.

The places and programs profiled in this chapter are examples of the role that deliberation and engagement play in putting a community in a position for success. First, in these communities evidence shows that education, dialogue, and deliberation can make the public more aware of the seriousness of local problems and can build their capacity to address those problems. Second, greater public involvement encourages a culture of collaboration, which not only solicits citizen participation but also encourages and expects it. In turn, the public requests and accepts responsibility for helping solve community challenges. Finally, collaborative community problem solving can harness the energy and enthusiasm of citizens working together, putting their talents to work to address problems, and at the same time, can promote a sense of ownership over the processes and outcomes of democratic community life.

So where do citizens turn when they want to participate? The formation of this public system of democracy can begin in local libraries, in nonprofit organizations, through regional agencies, through historical associations, in city hall, or via the Internet—in any organization or vehicle that can provide information and a public space for people to practice deliberative democracy with each other. Two national organizations—the National Issues Forums Institute and Everyday Democracy—provide issue discussion guides and a tested methodology to help communities develop deliberative dialogues. Citizens want to and must know how to deliberate and act on the issues important to them. It is not just good and open government, it is democracy.

CHAPTER SIX

Preserving the Past

The most difficult community stories to tell or remember are about the buildings and places that have been lost over the years. Part of our national culture and memory has found its way to the junkyard or the brickyard in the name of progress. Historic downtowns paid the price of modernization: the explosion of auto and air travel, an exodus to the suburbs and mall shopping, and an historic cognitive dissonance.

One of the most interesting aspects of asking questions about communities is that you get unexpected answers. Invariably, responses to revitalization questions turned to what was lost as well as what was saved. In a conversation about preservation, one local historian commented that citizens in her community still lament the loss of the "ridge." The mountain ridge framed her city until the early 1950s, when the desire to be the first city in the state to connect to the interstate highway system caused one end of the ridge to be destroyed and with it a beautiful residential and environmental area. Many people are still sorry and say so. For other communities, it is the loss of a movie theater, a train station, or an historic home.

To the chagrin of preservationists, the defining characteristics of towns and cities are gone forever. Even less-distinguished buildings, plazas, and courtyards are now the daily resting places for thousands of commuter cars. Action of any kind—dismantling of downtowns, creating large sports edifices, and the dissection of communities through urban renewal—was often sold to the public as a necessity caused by the urgency of the problem or situation.

Loss of identity was the price paid. Citizens in San Antonio grimace when they think about how in 1926 their treasured Riverwalk had to be saved from its designated fate as a paved-over storm sewer!

However, the National Preservation Act passed in 1986 began to change our minds and our landscapes. The Act has been instrumental in preventing the destruction of important buildings, homes, and cultural sites throughout the United States, but many important cultural sites were lost before it came to be. Given so many mistakes, it is easy to understand why some places need to make a fresh start. Balancing progress and preservation always has been a challenge and continues today.

This chapter illustrates how communities can use their past to positively affect their future. This is more than the restoration of buildings; it is about a broader concept of *owning the past* and using it to positively inform decision making. It is also about including a wide array of interest groups, often with conflicting goals and ideas, to cooperate and coalesce around the same vision.

Lowell's historic mills and Birmingham's Civil Rights Institute and District both provide opportunities to re-create history as a pathway for education and understanding in the community's past and future. Denver's Lower Downtown has been a boon to its economy and a magnate for sports, entertainment, and downtown living by preserving its "birthplace." Charlottesville, Virginia, tried an experiment thirty-five years ago to preserve its historic downtown. Today, it is the focal point of the community.

Increased Property Values and Increased Tourism

It is widely accepted that civic beauty and pride in community heritage are benefits often associated with historic preservation, but more and more researchers are beginning to take note of the economic advantages of preservation. A study done by Rypkema, Cheong, and Mason (2011) showed that there is still much to learn about the correlation between economic development and historic preservation, but their research identified five ways to measure impact: 1) creation of jobs and increased household income through construction, suppliers, and recreation or tourism jobs; 2) property value increase because of location within a historic district; 3) heritage tourism resulting from the "draw" of certain sites and locations; 4) environmental impact from saving sites and improving energy conservation; and 5) downtown commercial revitalization and historic preservation.

Historic preservation, downtown revitalization, and adaptive reuse benefit the entire community as well as particular segments, such as businesses, merchants, and homeowners. Designating a particular neighborhood or district as an historic place can enhance property values and resale opportunities for individual home owners. A report by the Michigan State Historic Preservation Office notes that "the stabilizing influence and protection that a historic district provides also may encourage private investment and increase property tax revenues for local governments" (Michigan Historic Preservation Network, 2002). In this way, the benefits that individual home owners reap from preservation may spill over and affect the community as a whole, leading to aesthetic improvements in historic districts as well as greater local tax revenues, according to the National Trust for Historic Preservation.

It is no secret that historic sites, structures, and landscapes are popular tourist attractions. Heritage and cultural tourism has become more popular since the early 1990s, as Americans seek to combine recreation with educational experiences that teach them about local and national history. A 2012 survey by the Travel Industry Association found that 81 percent of American adult travelers included at least one arts, heritage, or cultural activity on a trip; this translates into almost 118 million travelers per year. The travel and tourism industry reports that it is a top-ten employer in forty-eight states and the District of Columbia. The industry added 7 percent of all new jobs in 2011 (U.S. Travel Association, 2012). In addition, research has found that vacationers who visit historic sites tend to stay longer and spend more money than other types of travelers (National Trust for Historic Preservation, 2013).

History has shown that saving a building, a landmark, or even a neighborhood can anchor a place in untold ways. It has been said that a city without old buildings is like a person without a memory. Sometimes the benefits of historic property are strictly economic, but in other cases there are indirect uses that prove equally as important to community members and tourists alike. A

2011 report on historic preservation documented the economic power of preservation in specific terms. *The Economic Power of Heritage and Place* found that for every $1 million spent on preservation, thirty-two new jobs are created. Since 1981, Colorado has generated thirty-five thousand jobs and generated $2.5 billion in economic impact from historic preservation (Clarion Associates, 2011). More than that, property values in designated historic districts doubled and, in some cases, far more than doubled. The current Denver mayor, Michael Hancock, gave his views of historic preservation in 2011 that go beyond just economics:

> Historic preservation is part of the fabric of our city and greatly contributes to our quality of life. . . . Having a good quality of life is the most important contributor to the economic well-being of a city. We also know that there is a thriving historic tourism industry as a result of our preservation efforts. Denver maintains a rich history and, by protecting our diverse neighborhoods, we can ensure a good quality of life and economic strength for years to come. (Historic Denver, 2011)

The Intersection of Place, History, and Demand

Among the best-known and most economically successful forms of historic preservation are downtown revitalization campaigns. For instance, the Main Street Program, established by the National Trust for Historic Preservation in 1980, demonstrates that downtown revitalization can be an important component of the economic renewal of cities, towns, and neighborhoods, as Boston has demonstrated in the first citywide Main Street Program. Existing infrastructure downtown means that communities need not build new streets or water and sewer lines and thus allows the investments to be made in the buildings and amenities. Downtowns often are still the greatest employment sectors within cities, serve as incubators for new business, and are the focal points for businesses and residents in the city and in some instances the whole region (Tyler, 2000, p. 171). Not the least important, downtown revitalization may address growing concerns about land use and suburban sprawl. Rypkema (1994) pointed out that more intensive use of buildings and sites already in place may be one of the most effective methods of preventing sprawl. In her book *The End of the Suburbs* (2013), Gallagher argues that the trend out of cities is reversing. In 2011 the rate of population growth in urban centers outpaced the suburbs for the first time in a century. Rather than giving up on older neighborhoods or downtowns, which some businesses and residents abandoned years ago, renewal efforts build on existing assets and are bringing back young families, Millennials, and seniors to downtown living. Preservation efforts generally encourage communities to recognize that they have design options other than strip malls and high-rise office buildings; older buildings can be more interesting architecturally and culturally.

A successful economy development strategy for neighborhoods and their older buildings is *adaptive reuse*. Apart from aesthetic and historical considerations, demolishing existing buildings and constructing new ones is a costly proposition vis-à-vis the labor, materials, and craftsmanship needed for new construction projects. Rehabilitation is often seen as an expensive option, but studies have found that rehabilitation costs per square foot are often significantly less than the costs of new construction (Tyler, 2000, p. 185).

The adaptive reuse approach takes advantage of existing structures that might otherwise be destroyed and transforms them for alternative uses. Currently the federal government and thirty-one states encourage private investment in historic buildings by offering tax credits for rehabilitation, giving businesses an incentive to preserve rather than destroy (Schwartz, 2013). In Cincinnati, a study on the conversion of five buildings into downtown lofts found that for every $1 million spent on tax credits, eighty construction jobs were created and $8 million was spent on construction (Cleveland State University, 2011). Aside from its economic advantages, the adaptive reuse approach benefits the environment: the National Trust for Historic Preservation dubs it "the ultimate recycling." Homes, schools, churches, department stores, and even funeral homes have been repurposed.

Partly from vision and partly from necessity, many communities have initiated processes to reimagine their futures in response to negative changes that have occurred. Places that were once manufacturing hubs are now looking for their niche in the new economy. Often blessed with a built environment that reflects the resources of their manufacturing or commercial heydays, communities have libraries, art museums, historic homes, music venues, unused waterfronts, factories, and so forth that have helped define new identities. The tobacco warehouses in Richmond, Virginia's Shockoe Slip historic area are an example of this strategy. Today these bear little resemblance to their former use except in name. The American Cigar and the Lucky Strike apartment and condominium complexes now house singles, families, and retail in the high-ceiling structures once packed high with tobacco leaves.

While this transformation looks perfectly sensible in hindsight, how was the vision realized? How did demand generate the supply? In essence, it required identifying the intersection between place, history, and demand. This requires thinking of the asset in terms of location, physical dimensions, past use, and present currency. According to one builder, they simply looked at the demographic trends. The growth of a large urban university with a medical complex brought with it students and faculty who wanted to change the pattern of their parents and live downtown rather than in the suburbs. For the local planners, Shockoe Slip was a neighborhood juxtaposed to the downtown commercial area that could be an anchor for redevelopment. It had the architecture, the proximity to the state capital and government buildings, the James River and its views, and a hearty stock of unused buildings and some vacant land—the perfect storm of urban redesign. Hundreds of apartments and condominiums now exist in the area along with the businesses that support them. In 2009 the first of five former 1911 cold-storage warehouses were renovated for apartments with development offset by historic tax credits. These renewed assets have proved to be a win-win for the city and the neighborhood and provided a pathway for a different range of planning and development opportunities.

Planning professionals and citizens are moving beyond the status quo to a larger vision of buildings and places that actually fuels the demands of the new economy. The use and disposition of vacant public school buildings is a case in point. Viewed historically as the mark of an emerging neighborhood, local public schools signal the population growth or decline of an area. Places where demographics are changing are looking at the emerging opportunity to reuse the vacant school buildings left empty as the result of population change, consolidation, or modernization.

In a report from The Pew Charitable Trusts, *Shuttered Public Schools: The Struggle to Bring Old Buildings to Life*, Dowdall and Warner (2013) found that of the twelve school districts profiled in the report, 267 properties had been sold, leased, or repurposed since 2005. There were another 301 available buildings still standing vacant. While 40 percent of the repurposed buildings have gone to charter schools, other uses include market-rate and affordable housing, targeted services for individuals on both ends of the age spectrum, technology centers and business incubators, and cultural centers. The footprint of these buildings lends itself to a multitude of uses that can meet the goals of communities. Many have theatres; almost all have cafeterias, gymnasiums, and playing fields. A fair number of schools are architecturally or historically significant and qualify for historic tax credits. An article in *Atlantic Cities* calls for vacant properties to be used as places that could meet some of the needs of the nation's housing crisis, particularly for the homeless population (Erickson, 2012). There are estimates of five vacant buildings for every homeless person in America. Closed hospitals, shuttered factories, and boarded-up downtowns are both a challenge and a potential opportunity to retrofit the built environment in new ways. Lowell, Massachusetts, took adaptive reuse to a new level when the core of the city was designated a park by the National Park Service.

Links to Our Community and to Our Past

Saving and restoring older structures has a number of benefits other than purely economic ones. It does not take an architect or a designer to recognize that older structures often are more aesthetically pleasing than newer ones. The National Trust for Historic Preservation notes that some older buildings are "a gift to the street" because their style, texture, material, and charm—and perhaps even eccentricity—enrich and enliven their surroundings. Historic places contribute to a unique sense of community identity, character, and beauty that, once demolished, cannot be re-created.

Perhaps most important, historic sites, structures, and districts link a community to its past, promoting a sense of community consciousness and connectedness that high-rise office buildings and parking garages simply cannot. By protecting reminders of the past and safeguarding a community's heritage, preservation makes history available to future generations. Vibrant downtowns, lush landscapes, and historic structures tell a story that reminds a community of where it has been and maintains a sense of identity over time. One report warns that without historic preservation efforts, "History will be relegated to the occasional museum visit, and only acknowledged by those residents or visitors interested enough to seek it out. However, by engaging in serious preservation efforts, community leaders can ensure that the past has a constant presence and is not forgotten" (Price, 2005). History and tradition can be a region's greatest cultural and economic assets, and their unique character makes them irreplaceable.

Historic preservation is a smart investment vis-à-vis aesthetic beauty, economic development, and community identity. It can instill civic pride, generate tourism, revitalize downtowns, and educate citizens about their local heritage (Virginia Department of Historic Resources, 2013). The attractiveness of a glitzy urban center or a quaint small town may seem less important when compared with challenges such as affordable housing or the quality of public education. Community leaders must weigh the different options for investments that can make a community strong and attractive; it's never a cut-and-dried decision. Fortunately, communities often do not need to choose between preservation and economic development. Preservation can provide economic as well as civic and cultural benefits for all kinds of communities. Buildings, museums, and historic districts help people learn. They can be magnets for recreational clusters. They are visible reminders of days and times gone by. They bind people in a shared, if not common, set of circumstances.

Lowell, Massachusetts: The Spindle City

Long known as the Spindle City, the charting of Lowell's rise and fall as an industrial city is really the story of the Industrial Revolution in the United States. For much of the nineteenth century—from 1826 until the 1890s—Lowell was among the largest and most impressive industrial cities in the world. Innovations in corporate structure and industrial technology kept Lowell at the forefront of the American industrial scene well into the 1900s. The flight of textile corporations to the South for cheaper, unorganized labor, beginning in the 1920s, dealt the communities of the Northeast and Midwest a blow from which some have never recovered. By 1926, a rash of closures and relocations left only three of the original textile corporations operating in Lowell.

The Depression hit Lowell hard, and total textile employment dropped from a high of twenty-two thousand in 1924 to eight thousand in 1936. Some mill complexes were torn down or allowed to slide into disrepair. World War II brought brisk demand for cloth, and the remaining mills did well during those years. Remington, General Electric, and U.S. Rubber competed with the Amers, Merrimack, and Boott textile companies for workers, so conditions improved and wages tripled. The year 1945 brought an economic downturn, however, as defense contract money dried up; the Boott and Merrimack mills finally closed in the 1950s. Many mill boardinghouses were razed, as was the old tenement neighborhood of Little Canada. The empty century-old factories stood as looming and sometimes unwelcome reminders of the Lowell of the past. Young people were leaving, and those who stayed "were ambivalent about their history, recalling the hard conditions under which their parents had worked" (Lowell National Historical Park, 2013). In the 1970s civic leaders began to form a challenging new vision of Lowell. The condition of the city at the time of the Bicentennial was pretty grim. Unemployment was at the highest level in Massachusetts and one of the highest levels in the United States at 10 percent. Young people and skilled workers were making a fast exit. Some people labeled the city as "hopeless," and still others thought the historic mills would look better as parking lots!

However, the superintendent of Lowell Public Schools, Patrick Mogan, was one of the civic leaders who insisted that a revitalization effort be based on Lowell's industrial and ethnic heritage. Mogan believed that Lowell's distinguished past as the centerpiece for the Industrial Revolution in America could be used to reinvigorate the community, stimulate the economy, and improve the educational system. "Lowell had a low image of itself," according to Martha Mayo, head of the Center for Lowell History. "Pat Mogan and others had the notion of using the city as a classroom to improve self-esteem." A major component of the plan was the creation of an historical park, which would showcase the city as a living museum and provide a springboard for redevelopment. Lowell was considered to be the first major American city built for the needs of production (Frenchman and Lane, 2008).

The Lowell Plan and the Lowell Development and Finance Corporation changed the course of Lowell's path from a community of decline to one of rebirth. This group first enlisted the support of the local government, winning endorsement from the city council in 1972. The Lowell Heritage State Park emerged in 1974 from this cooperative effort. The effort did not stop there. Both Paul Tsongas and Edward Kennedy, then senators from Massachusetts, also supported the initiative. In 1978, after several years of study and hearings on the plan, Lowell National Historical Park was created along with the Lowell Preservation Commission. The National Park Service was charged with stabilizing, cataloguing, and interpreting Lowell's past. The Preservation Commission faced a similar challenge: stabilizing and restoring the massive physical infrastructure of historical Lowell. As the park would be situated in the heart of downtown Lowell, it was clear that the larger mission of the Park Service presence in Lowell would be to restore and encourage private redevelopment of the city. "What occurred was not just redevelopment," remembers Mayo, "but really the coming together of four circles of action: the preservation community, the federal Model Cities program, the city planning office, and the congressional delegation." At the same time, educational opportunities in Lowell improved, with the University of Lowell's formation (now the University of Massachusetts Lowell) from the merger of Lowell State College and Lowell Technological Institute in 1975 (Lowell National Historical Park, 2013) and the opening of Middlesex Community College in the city.

Lowell had a dramatic transformation during the following decade. Overall one hundred old buildings were rehabilitated, including the Boott and Merrimack mills complexes and the old Bon Marché department store on the historic Merrimack Street in downtown. Wang Laboratories, a major international high-tech firm, built a new facility and leased space in one of the major mill complexes for its hardware production and distribution facilities. The National Park Service located its Visitor Center in part of another mill complex and partnered with the city and a housing development corporation to rehabilitate the rest of the complex for residences and offices. At the Boott Cotton Mills complex, the Park Service took over about a third of the former mill for its museum and park offices. The University of Massachusetts Lowell collaborated with the Park Service to run the Tsongas Industrial History Center, an educational, hands-on learning center for school groups, on several floors of the Boott Cotton Mills complex. The rest of the complex has been redeveloped as office and ware-house space and planned housing. One of the few remaining boardinghouses, once serving New England farm girls who came to work the looms between 1836 and the 1940s, became the Park Service's Boardinghouse Exhibit and was connected to the newly constructed Mogan Cultural Center, housing the University of Massachusetts Lowell's Center for Lowell History and serving as rehearsal and performance space for a number of cultural organizations.

The dream of a revitalized community that was envisioned more than three decades ago has become, through careful plan-ning and determined work, the hub of redevelopment through-out the city. According to Mayo, people are finding Lowell a very attractive community. The park is credited with transforming the image of the city as a "good place to locate and do business" as opposed to other cities in the region. In the end, the most signifi-cant contribution was its role in helping to build a diverse economy. "Pat Mogan's early vision for Lowell was to be a 'good address.' This is no longer a slogan, it is reality" (Frenchman and Lane, 2008, p. 10).

Birmingham: Owning the Past and Telling the Story

In 2012 the Birmingham Civil Rights District was named as the Attraction of the Year by the Alabama Tourism Department. The district includes the Birmingham Civil Rights Institute (BCRI), Kelly Ingram Park, and the 16th Street Baptist Church. "The historic Civil Rights District was ground zero for the 1963 civil rights campaign, which turns fifty in 2013," the Alabama Tourism Department said in a statement announcing the award. "With the opening of the Birmingham Civil Rights Institute in 1992, the city found a place to tell its story" (Watkins, 2012).

Birmingham, Alabama, was historically an industrial city that drew its strength, wealth, and resources first from its rich veins of iron ore and then from steel. Founded in the mid-nineteenth century, the Birmingham area grew, rapidly reaching a population of four hundred thousand by 1930. It had two nicknames: the "Magic City" because it grew from a small town to a big city almost overnight and the "Pittsburgh of the South" because of its steel-making prowess (Norrell, 1993, pp. 177–178). However, Birmingham's real notoriety came in the 1960s, when it became the focus of the Civil Rights movement. The focal point for the movement was Kelly Ingram Park, a popular place for families to gather near the African American business district and just across the street from the 16th Street Baptist Church.

White resistance to integration was fierce. The Reverend Fred Shuttlesworth, a local pastor and head of the Alabama Christian Movement for Human Rights, invited Martin Luther King Jr. and the Southern Christian Leadership Conference staff to assist in the Birmingham movement. However, a Sunday morning in September 1963 changed Birmingham and the world forever. A bomb was placed in the 16th Street Baptist Church, killing four young African American girls. The world mourned Birmingham Sunday. Birmingham was seen as the center of racism and segregation. After a visit to the Holocaust Museum in Jerusalem, former mayor David Vann proposed a resolution to the city council to establish a civil rights museum. Political leaders led by Vann and then-mayor Richard Arrington sought to create a civil rights museum as a center for reconciliation in the late 1970s. The resolution passed unanimously in 1979. Vann, law clerk to Justice Black when the *Brown v. Board of Education* decision was handed down, remembered that the project "did not meet with instantaneous success" (Gates, 2002, p. 17). Part of the resistance was embarrassment and shame, but a part also was comprised of vestiges of the past. It was difficult to get white leaders to visibly identify with the museum. Naysayers said that such a place would open up old wounds, reinforce the negative impression about Birmingham, and be a harborer of troublemakers; last but not least, no whites would come to the museum, recalled Odessa Woolfolk, president emeritus of the Birmingham Civil Rights Institute. These prevailing sentiments made the launch of the project, to remember and learn from the past, rocky and tenuous. However, the supporters were inspired to do something positive about Birmingham's history, and they kept at it.

It took seven more years for Mayor Richard Arrington, the first African American mayor since Reconstruction, to see the idea of a museum become a reality. A diverse task force was appointed, which included Vann and Woolfolk, then director of urban affairs at the University of Alabama in Birmingham, as chair. The first step was to raise funds. A $65 million city bond issue was first proposed in 1986, with $10 million to go to the creation of the museum; it failed twice in two years. There was a sentiment that given the depressed economy, Birmingham needed other things more. There was a real concern that a visible reminder of the past would further damage Birmingham's image. Although the African American community supported the museum overall, some objected that there was a lack of representation of "foot soldiers" in the effort. In addition, some people—white and African American—didn't see a need for a museum. But Arrington and others were not deterred (Gates, 2002, p. 20).

The final funding breakthrough came from the Historic Preservation Authority, which issued an $8 million bond, and from capital generated from a city land swap. A group of white and black businesspeople formed a task force to raise additional funds from the corporate community. Even after the money was raised, according to Woolfolk, the dissension continued: "Some people felt that the money could be used to fix potholes, fund public works projects, or improve the schools." The corporate community, by contrast, had come around. The fundraising campaign yielded $4.2 million—$1 million more than the goal. There was a sense that the museum was the right civic thing to do, says Woolfolk.

The Birmingham Civil Rights Institute (BCRI) opened in 1992 to a fanfare of local, national, and international visitors; Odessa Woolfolk became the founding president. It was designed to tell the story of the past, but it also was to be a center for human rights for the present and the future. It has become a national and international center for reconciliation and human rights. Bishop Desmond Tutu has stated that it was the Birmingham struggle that inspired the people of South Africa.

The location of the institute is important. It sits across the street from the 16th Street Baptist Church and Kelly Ingram Park. The church was a symbol of the movement. The park was the central gathering place in the 1960s, where so many citizens and foot soldiers were arrested. The entire area surrounding the institute has been designated as the Civil Rights District.

The contents of the institute are real, not sugarcoated. They include the jail cell that once held Martin Luther King Jr., Fred Shuttlesworth's Bible, a Ku Klux Klan robe, a copy of *Brown v. Board of Education* signed by all nine justices, school desks, papers, photos, and even a bus of the same vintage as one ridden by the Freedom Riders.

The institute has helped Birmingham own the past. Thousands of people from over a hundred countries and of all races have visited the institute. A decade after its founding, Woolfolk said, "The Institute recognizes the redemptive importance of memory. It is both a time capsule and a modern-day think tank focused on seeking equitable solutions to common problems" (Birmingham Civil Rights Institute, 2002). The institute is a place not only for understanding the history of the past but also for making history. A curriculum has been developed with an emphasis on human rights. Programs for schoolchildren help them to understand the effects of racism and prejudice. It is a place for learning about the richness of the arts, culture, and heritage of Birmingham's African American community.

The institute has established international alliances with Israel and South Africa. Archbishop Desmond Tutu and the last apartheid-era president F. W. de Klerk, both Nobel Peace Prize winners, came to Birmingham in 2002. Close collaborations with the Mandela House in Soweto township and the Apartheid Museum in Johannesburg led to visits to South Africa in 2011. As part of the International Youth Legacy Leadership initiative at the institute, ten young people from each country participated in exchange visits to learn from their collective experiences from visiting the sites of memory and struggle-related museums in the United States and South Africa (Anderson, 2013).

The Birmingham Civil Rights Institute is not just a museum or an educational institution: it is a major step forward for a community that must remember its past in order to re-create its future. With premier medical facilities, research centers, and higher education institutions, Birmingham is moving forward on many fronts. The institute is an important piece of the mosaic that includes Birmingham's past and future.

No More Just Knocking Down or Paving Over

Experience has taught us that there should be enforced guidelines for the decision-making process for demolishing buildings of historical significance. In some cases, the buildings that should be saved are not on the historical register. Rather, they hold important cultural, social, *and* historical significance to the fabric of the community. There must be a waiting period. Communities must have enough cooling-off time so that decisions are not bulldozed (literally and figuratively) through the system. Why rush? Finally, there should be a broad-based committee, including local government, business, and citizens—from throughout the community—that considers the opportunity costs of losing buildings, green space, and even stands of trees. These are irreplaceable things that need attention and thought. Communities need a process of deciding about the fate of older structures as much or more than they need a process of deciding about new development.

People still want to remember the familiar. Historic and cultural places can be research centers, public history museums, and gateways to new economic opportunities. Downtowns also provide a public space where people can develop and renew their sense of community and place. The examples that follow show the patience required to realize the vision for downtowns that encourage this renewal: Charlottesville, Virginia; Asheville, North Carolina; and Denver, Colorado.

Charlottesville: A World-Class City

In the 1980s, downtown Charlottesville, Virginia, looked bleak. Anchor stores were moving to the suburban mall, and small businesses were closing their doors. In 1984 Charlottesville embarked on a downtown revitalization effort that can provide lessons for all communities interested in renewing the health and viability of their downtowns. Located in the foothills of the Blue Ridge Mountains in central Virginia, Charlottesville (population 50,000 in the city and about 150,000 in the surrounding county of Albemarle) is home to a number of historical sites that attract thousands of visitors every year, including Thomas Jefferson's Monticello, James Monroe's Ash Lawn-Highland, James Madison's Montpelier, and the grounds of the University of Virginia. These attractions notwithstanding, in the late 1960s Charlottesville found itself facing many of the same problems confronting cities throughout the country: rapid suburbanization and the accompanying erosion of the central commercial and residential urban core. Retail sales in the central business district and real property assessments were down, and one consultant plan recommended that 65 percent of downtown buildings be rehabilitated or replaced because they had deteriorated or were obsolete. Early attempts at urban renewal and rounds of planning had come to naught (Lucy, 2002, p. 9).

The city refused to abandon its hope for downtown renewal. Alvin Clements, who chaired a commission that considered how to deal with the deterioration of the downtown from 1971 to 1976, reveals the philosophy that guided Charlottesville's leaders during this crossroads in the community's history: "We thought downtown renovation was necessary, because it was the heart. If it went bad, the rest of the city would go with it" (Lucy, 2002, p. 9). With a firm commitment to the idea of downtown revitalization, city government enthusiastically spearheaded the revitalization effort. Charlottesville officials pored over reports from national consultants and began to implement a series of policies and concepts suggested by the consultants. The reports called on Charlottesville to create a downtown that would be clean, safe, and auto free, in order to encourage people to use the space for work, leisure, and entertainment. Throughout the revitalization process, public and private partnerships and citizen engagement provided needed capital, creative energy, and commitment. Put simply, the common goal was to make downtown Charlottesville a place where people would want to be.

After more than thirty-five years of thoughtful planning, investor support, and citizen participation, that goal undeniably has been achieved. As soon as the city made a commitment to downtown revitalization, the work began. A new parking garage was built; office buildings, restaurants, and shops opened; and new downtown housing was constructed. Private investments poured into the downtown area, and gross business receipts rose dramatically. Preservation was a key element of the master plan submitted by the consulting firm Lawrence Halprin & Associates in 1974, which stated that "the quality of character, scale, and texture of the older structures in downtown was a unique possession well worth maintaining" (Lucy, 2002, p. 36). Buildings that had been vacated were not abandoned but were preserved and transformed for alternative uses, including an elementary school that became an art center, a post office that was transformed into a library, and an auto repair shop that eventually became the headquarters of a local television station. After being blocked twice in the late 1970s, efforts to create a historic preservation district along the pedestrian mall were successful in 1984. Buildings were going to be protected. Concern for historic preservation guided decisions about the construction and character of the downtown mall. A design scheme featuring a tight grid, small blocks, and narrow streets created a pedestrian-friendly environment and a fifteen-block auto-free zone—quite significant for a city of Charlottesville's size.

A task force composed of city officials and downtown business-people gave design guidelines to downtown businesses that limited colors and materials to those thought compatible with the character of the buildings, helping to create an attractive and aesthetically pleasing setting. Not least important, the community itself valued preservation as a desirable approach to design and renewal. As one report put it, "Preservation and adaptive use are processes that can be encouraged with local ordinances and administrative procedures. But local culture and values probably contribute more to success" (Lucy, 2002, p. 38).

The most visible manifestation of downtown Charlottesville's philosophy of preservation was the construction of the pedestrian mall beginning in 1976. The tree-lined mall has a number of restaurants, bookstores, and cafés and is frequented by street musicians, vendors, and strolling families. The mall is anchored by a hotel and an indoor ice-skating rink on one end and by an amphitheater on the other.

The success of Charlottesville's downtown revitalization would not have been possible without collaboration between the city and other groups, including private investors, businesses, nonprofit organizations, and citizens and its commitment to preserve the historic character of the downtown. The city's decision to take a leadership role in downtown revitalization, however, was a critical first step in encouraging other community members to come on board. Tackling the revitalization project with persistence and enthusiasm, city leadership gave private groups and citizens the confidence that downtown revitalization was a process that it would remain committed to for the long term.

Alvin Clements pointed out that "getting city government to take a major role was very controversial . . . Many thought downtown was a business problem, not a problem for government" (Lucy, 2002, p. 78). But it was precisely the role of government that jump-started the revitalization effort. Citizen participation, too, has been a Charlottesville tradition since revitalization efforts began in the early 1970s. Citizen involvement has taken many forms over the years, including citizens' commissions, public meetings and roundtable discussions, planning and design task forces, and public hearings.

A final element in the success of downtown Charlottesville has been the timing of the city government's decisions. Because the revitalization project began before downtown department stores relocated in suburban shopping malls, the loss of those stores was anticipated and occurred after the transition to a new downtown had already begun. By the time the major anchor stores had departed for outlying areas in Albemarle County, the evolution of downtown to a center for entertainment, specialty shops, cultural experiences, business, and civic life was already under way. In this way, city leaders addressed a situation—the growing attraction of retailers to suburban shopping malls—before it became a problem in their city. Smart communities invest in the prevention of problems through planning, analysis, and foresight that can allow them to address challenges before they become full-blown crises. In Charlottesville, "The department store exodus did not lead to panic," one report concludes. "In a sense, it was an expected part of the plan" (Lucy, 2002, p. 35).

By all accounts the last thirty-five years have realized the vision for downtown Charlottesville. Thousands of people flock to the downtown mall throughout the week but particularly at night and on weekends. Music and the arts are a big part of the draw. There are regular music venues as well as an outdoor pavilion at one end of the downtown mall and two historic theatres that host live music, theatre, opera, and specialty shows. Collectively, these three places had 250,000 attendees in 2012.

Downtown Charlottesville remains a success today because the city, private investors, and the public made a commitment to preserve the area's historical assets. Downtown has experienced several new investments in recent years that have built on the strong foundation already in place. The community refers to itself as a world-class city, and it is certainly on the right track. Charlottesville's downtown renaissance did not take place overnight. Having set realistic goals and implemented plans to achieve them, community members were able to watch the revitalization of downtown Charlottesville unfold over many years—and they were rewarded for their patience.

Asheville: The Jewel in the Mountains

Asheville, North Carolina, was cited by Richard Florida as the eleventh of 124 cities on his creativity index ranking of cities under 250,000 in population (Florida, 2002). This designation only begins to reveal the creative economy that Asheville is generating in its modern-day renaissance. A city of almost seventy thousand, it is a city of contrasts: strong religious values and dedicated work ethic juxtaposed with free expression, inclusiveness, and a thriving downtown hub. Asheville has found its rhythm. However, it has not always been so good. Asheville's modern development began around the turn of the twentieth century. It was the resort destination of grand hotels, health resorts, and spas. It had more than fifty boardinghouses, as depicted by Thomas Wolfe in *Look Homeward, Angel.* Asheville's population grew from about four thousand in the late-nineteenth century to more than fifty thousand 25 years later. Clearly, it was a city on the move, with thousands of tourists and a growing year-round population (Ready, 1986, p. 78).

The city was bursting at the seams with real estate speculation, physical expansion, heavy borrowing, and a growing population in the 1920s. About that time, the real estate market began to slide, and when the Great Depression hit in 1930, Asheville became one of its worst victims. At 9 A.M. on November 9, 1930, the city's four major banks closed. Unfortunately, Asheville's leadership had spent tremendous sums to improve the city's appearance in order to attract visitors and tourists. As early as 1922, tax revenues were declining, so the city issued and sold municipal bonds—more than $23 million worth. Asheville's debt in 1930 was higher than that of Raleigh, Durham, Winston-Salem, and Greensboro combined, and the city could not meet its obligations. Through a restructuring plan, the city did not go bankrupt, and future indebtedness was limited by severely constraining municipal spending. It took Asheville until 1976 to repay its Depression debt—forty-six years (Ready, 1986, p. 88).

During that almost half century, there were significant public works projects on the Blue Ridge Parkway, so Asheville fared better than many places. As Herbert Miles wrote in the *Asheville Citizen-Times*, "Have faith in yourself, . . . in Asheville, . . . and . . . have patience. Let us pay the piper for we have danced! And we shall dance again" (Ready, 1986 p. 92). They certainly tried, but times were very hard. In fact, the bitter memories of Asheville's quest to become "the Queen City of the Mountains" scared and angered citizens—they had seen and heard too much. For more than forty years, political campaigns focused on preventing annexation, consolidation, or cooperation with the county. For all intents and purposes, the 1970s saw Asheville at a standstill, except for the dollars invested by the Appalachian Regional Commission in the interstate highway system, the location of federal and state agencies in Asheville, and outside investments in urban development and health care. These changes began to lure locals back to the city. Ever present was a strong preservation effort, a thriving artistic community, and a wealth of beautiful architecture.

There was no urban renewal to speak of in the 1950s and 1960s. Many projects just could not get off the ground without public indebtedness. However, with the debt paid off, Asheville finally could look to the future. As early as 1977, the city council created the Asheville Revitalization Commission, charged with the physical, economic, and cultural development of the central business district. As the commission's report on the community reflected, "Asheville, the City in the Land of the Sky, can continue its slow, easy path of following the lead of other cities—doing some good things, some bad things, or just doing nothing—or it can strike out on its own path. Preserving and building a uniquely livable city will not necessarily be the easiest path" (Asheville Revitalization Commission, 1978, pp. 11–12).

This participatory revitalization process identified four key aspects of Asheville's future development: livability, history, uniqueness, and accessibility. The future was just beginning, and it looked very good. Asheville had much to build on in the downtown. In fact, downtown Asheville has the second-largest number of Art Deco buildings in the Southeast, following only by Miami Beach. The urgency to reverse the vacancy trend generated a number of renewal options, including a proposed development plan that would have leveled eleven blocks in the center city, composed of a rich architectural fabric of Romanesque Revival, late Victorian, Neo-Gothic, Neo-Georgian, Classical Revival, and Art Deco styles.

The story of Asheville's restoration is one of citizen empowerment and old-fashioned tenacity. In 1980 the Asheville Revitalization Commission was ready to share the fruits of its hard labor with downtown businesses and the general public. With the help of an outside developer, the proposal was to level 11.5 acres of the downtown for an indoor shopping mall. In order not to raise the ire of the historical preservationists, the proposal called for razing the buildings but keeping the facades. The promise was a revitalized downtown that would lure suburban shoppers and rid the area of deteriorating buildings. The plan might have been approved had it not been for about twenty-five citizens who organized themselves as Save Downtown Asheville and vowed to fight what they felt was the desecration of a beautiful and potentially viable downtown. As Wayne Caldwell, one of the leaders, said, "It was a loose coalition of downtown business owners and citizens that grew into the Committee of 1000." The group had varying reasons for the opposition, ranging from the preservation of self-owned businesses, to historical preservation, to just-a-bad-idea advocates. On the other side of the fence was the Fact Finding Committee for the Urban Complex, composed of most of the key business leaders, who saw the redevelopment plan as the only way to save downtown Asheville. The line in the sand was clearly drawn.

Despite loud objections by the Committee of 1000, endless discussions, and presentations at weekly city council meetings, a decision was made to hold a referendum to finance the project with local revenue bonds. The Committee of 1000 campaigned hard against the measure. The bond issue failed two to one. Ashevillians were saying not only "no" to the project, but also "no" to any more borrowing for expansion. Too many remembered 1930.

After the vote, the mayor appointed a group to look at alternative downtown development. The result, although not linear or easy, was a move to revitalize Asheville, keeping its small-town atmosphere and historical buildings. It was an uphill battle. In 1991, 80 percent of the downtown was either empty or substandard. There was little residential occupancy in the city. To help middle- and lower-income people find housing in the city, the council earmarked one cent of a four-cent tax increase toward the Housing Trust Fund. The fund provided low-interest loans to developers who wanted to build affordable housing. Since the decision to save downtown, more than one hundred downtown buildings have been rehabilitated and developed with $200 million in private funds. Grove Arcade, originally built in 1929, has been restored and is two-thirds occupied with fifty-two businesses (Williams and Boyle, 2003, p. A5).

Asheville's future changed in 1981 because a group of citizens said "no." Their persistence has paid off. Today Asheville's downtown has almost 100 percent occupancy, and land values have risen dramatically. There are 230 downtown businesses operating at capacity. In 1982 the land values in all of the Central Business District totaled $48,237,500 (Anderson, Brown-Graham, and Lobenhofer, 2007). By 2010–2011, in the subsequent twenty years, the number had risen to $1,135,425,387 (Ha, 2011). As important, downtown Asheville has become a hub for the arts and cultural events. In 2012 tourism brought in $3.1 billion to the Asheville area.

Asheville is one of the creative and cultural centers of the South, with a preserved downtown that is the envy of most. It is bustling and thriving. A series of articles in January 2003 (Barrett, 2003; Williams and Boyle, 2003) in the *Asheville Citizen-Times* proclaimed downtown Asheville as "on the verge." But some people think it has gone beyond "the verge." Donovan Rypkema calls Asheville "one of the great success stories in America for a city that size" (Barrett, 2003, p. A14). There are some citizens sitting in cafés, running downtown businesses, and displaying their art in one of a hundred or more art galleries who might be saying, "We almost lost the opportunity." Asheville made a smart decision thanks to the efforts of a small group of citizens who refused to follow the pack. Interestingly enough, the series of articles in the *Citizen-Times* did not mention the opposition in the city—that's too bad. Even with the inevitable old wounds that still exist, it is important to understand how Asheville reclaimed its past. Community members were the owners and the authors of their future.

The leadership provided by the city, the private sector, and citizens has made all the difference in Asheville. The key to the positive outcome was a combination of access to federal and state dollars in the form of housing tax credits, focused local public leadership, a strong contingency of citizens, private sector partners, and "kaleidoscope thinking."

Denver: The Gold Mine Neighborhood

Denver, Colorado, has always had a prominent place in the American West. Long considered the financial, manufacturing, agricultural, and cultural hub from Kansas City west, it has developed a diverse economy that includes financial services, oil and gas, media, tourism, major sports, and high tech.

In the 1980s, the recession hit the Denver area hard—very hard. According to former mayor Federico Peña, it was the worst recession that the city and state had ever experienced. The bottom fell out of oil and gas prices, real estate values plummeted, and businesses and banks failed. By 1988, fourteen thousand energy-related jobs had been lost, 50 percent of the total energy workforce. The downtown office vacancy rate was at 31 percent, and people were looking for answers (Adams and Parr, 1997, pp. 78–80).

That answer came as Peña and others looked at the assets of the city and how they could be leveraged to stabilize and grow the economy. Obvious places to look were: location, natural beauty, tourism, and development opportunities in Lower Downtown and the Central Platte Valley. During this same time period, a group of eight people were thinking independently about the possibilities of and the need to protect Lower Downtown, the historic area of the city where Denver was born. This group of eight realized that Lower Downtown was a "gold mine as a neighborhood and the birthplace of Denver," says Lisa Purdy, at that time on the staff of the organization Historic Denver. It was not just selected buildings that were important but the whole collection. In the early 1980s, Lower Downtown was an aggregate of a few restaurants, low-rent hotels, and panhandlers. Buildings were beginning to be razed for parking lots to provide revenue for property owners. Renewed interest in the area occurred with a proposed plan to link the new convention center to the anchor building in the area, Union Station. Preservationists feared that putting a new convention center in Lower Downtown would cause the destruction of Denver's birthplace and the historic buildings.

Between 1981 and 1988, 20 percent of the buildings in the historic Lower Downtown area affectionately called LoDo were destroyed and the land used primarily for parking lots. This was of great concern to a small breakfast group of eight preservationists, Lower Downtown business owners, and developers, who hammered out a plan that included support for putting the convention center behind Union Station in exchange for stronger controls on the demolition of historic buildings. The executive director of the Denver Partnership (a downtown Denver booster group), upon hearing the plan, promptly said that this would never work; the group was too small to make such a controversial plan acceptable to a larger constituency. As Lisa Purdy, one of the principals, remembers, "I was really upset to hear this after all our hard work—but he was right." He suggested that Purdy join a new task force being convened by Mayor Peña. She was appointed as the "representative of the preservationists" to the new Downtown Area Committee. The twenty-eight-person committee was charged with developing a comprehensive plan for all of downtown, one part of which was Lower Downtown. Earlier in 1982 the city had provided incentives for Lower Downtown residential development with new zoning laws. However, a key piece was missing—demolition control—that is, who had the final say on which buildings went or stayed. That issue came to define the broader conversation as the process went forward (Collins, Waters, and Dotson, 1991, pp. 74–76).

The mayor's Downtown Area Plan Steering Committee completed its work in May 1986. The final plan included a comprehensive package of recommendations for Lower Downtown as well as other parts of downtown. It is important to note that it had been three years since the group of eight held their weekly breakfast meetings. As Purdy so aptly observed, "Tenacity is a very big element" in creating a vision and community change. Calling for creating distinctive districts throughout downtown Denver, the plan designated Lower Downtown for both preservation and reinvestment. However, it took another two-and-a-half years before the historic-district designation was adopted by the city council. Having a plan with recommendations was a far cry from an actual ordinance that put restrictions into legal form.

Hundreds of meetings took place, with property owners and preservationists looking for common ground. In 1988 the historic-district ordinance finally was passed and with it design standards on new construction, strict controls on the demolition of buildings, and a package of incentives for marketing plans for the area. Property owners and developers opposed the designation, but Mayor Peña's leadership throughout the planning process proved essential, and at this point pivotal. The mayor had been supportive of the Lower Downtown development since the conversation began. As he says, "[We felt that we] ought to combine history with growth. The old and new were part of our unique assets." However, as he and others remember, property owners and developers argued that the restrictions on design, use, and demolition infringed on their ownership rights and would limit their ability to make a profit. Peña countered this with assurances that the city not only would provide economic enhancements to the district, but also would step up infrastructure investment and law-enforcement presence, as well as create a loan fund and make streetscape improvements. The development of Lower Downtown was not smooth sailing. Opposition came from many sides, and even the preservationists disagreed at times. But the stalwart held firm. It was clear from other cities' experiences that there were some nonnegotiables in the process—a key one being demolition control. The mayor never wavered on this. The partnerships that were built throughout the process have stood the test of time. The collaborative nature of the Downtown Area Plan Steering Committee brought divergent and convergent ideas together in new ways. According to former mayor Peña, "Nothing works without partnerships" (Peña, 2003).

The story of Lower Downtown has evolved since 1988. The city followed through on its commitments and investments. A major league baseball stadium was built in the area with public-private funds, community development block grant money was provided for Lower Downtown loft housing, and property owners began to reinvest in the area. Even the chamber of commerce moved to Lower Downtown. In a report by Hammer, Siler, George Associates (1990), the authors said this of Lower Downtown: "The research and analysis suggest that virtually all of the change to date has been positive and will likely accelerate in coming years."

This prediction proved to be right. Before the historic designation, the area had a 40 percent vacancy rate, and 30 percent of the properties were in foreclosure (MacMahon, 2012). Today LoDo is teeming with visitors, has residents of all ages, and supports a thriving 24–7 culture. Vacancy rates are as low as 6 percent, and rents have doubled over the last year. It is considered one of the strongest markets in the city (Huspeni, 2013). A trip to watch the Colorado Rockies baseball team at Coors Field in Denver has become a destination for locals and visitors alike. Just a few decades ago, the stadium did not exist and neither did much of a future for the neighborhood where it now stands. The saving, restoration, and development of Lower Downtown in Denver is a sterling example of mayoral leadership, civic participation, and vision, but it was not easy or quick. These impressive results came after more than two decades of critical work and partnerships by all sectors. Positive decisions about preservation take time, need the input and thinking of many people from throughout the community, but in the end, prove to be really smart.

New Paradigms for Downtown

Downtown revitalization and preservation are not one-size-fits-all templates, and they don't often lend themselves to textbook analysis. Rather, says M. J. Brodie, president of the Baltimore Development Corporation, "Questions of urban development challenge traditional methods of planning and implementation, requiring new, sometimes radical—meaning 'from the root'—ideas, combining seemingly opposite or unrelated concepts into new paradigms, into synthesis of thought and action" (Brodie, 1997). Seven principles flow from this observation:

1. There must be an understandable physical vision—large enough to excite the imagination of all the participants, but structured enough that it can be achieved in the increments that realities of time and funding usually dictate.

2. The vision must be grounded in the authentic character of the place (its history, climate, terrain, cultural values) and informed by an articulated set of goals for the future—goals that describe what the city wants to be.

3. To implement the vision (the plan), a partnership must be formed between the public and private sectors, each sector bringing its skills to the process, to produce a better result than either could have achieved alone.

4. The public sector, through redeveloping the city's infrastructure (transportation, utilities, public open spaces), must set the stage for private investment.

5. A high level of quality must be set for design and construction (major redevelopment is often a once-in-a-generation opportunity!), in both public and private projects.

6. Methods must be developed to broaden the base of the redevelopment project, and to obtain not only cooperation but also enthusiasm from those involved.

7. A structure for implementation must be created that combines responsibility with necessary authority, that is results oriented and accountable to the citizens, and that is capable of guiding the process over an extended period of time. (Brodie, 1997)

Downtown revitalization and historic preservation are never an easy sell, but they can be done. Often the hardest step is the first one. In these cases, communities of different sizes and situations illustrate how Main Street or a museum or an historical district can be the key to a new community development strategy. In very different venues and under widely divergent circumstances, these cities all made decisions that built on values, history, and location. In each case, the revitalization itself was a secondary result of the larger accomplishment of citizen reinvestment—in one another and in the place where they live.

These illustrations weave a powerful story of partnership, citizen action, imagination, and honesty. Maybe that's what historic preservation really is at its core. In each case, the motivation for restoration went beyond economic development. The goal and the outcome were bigger than that. The key to these examples is that there was a vision of something beyond the buildings themselves. It had to do with learning, but also with remembering and respecting.

| Growing New Leaders

One of the smartest decisions ever made in North Carolina was the creation of the Research Triangle Institute and Park in 1959. It was made by a visionary group, including the governor, key business leaders, and the presidents and faculty of three universities: Duke University, North Carolina State University, and the University of North Carolina at Chapel Hill. The lessons from the creation of the Research Triangle Park certainly speak volumes about tenacity and vision, but they also speak about the kinds of imaginative leaders who could create something as big and bold as a research park in a state dominated at the time by low-wage manufacturing and agriculture.

Research Triangle Institute was officially created in late 1958, but it took years of commitment from the state, the universities, and the business community for the decision to bear real fruit. There were lean years in the 1980s when some companies backed out, and last-minute loans were required when funds got low. But the leadership, different by now from the original in some cases, stayed the course. The universities still compete mightily for students, for grants, and in athletics, but they all know that their collective futures have been well served by their willingness and ability to work together to develop a regional technology, research, and business park. Now almost a half-century later, what are the results of the visionary leadership from more than half a century ago? The Research Triangle Institute was the first occupant in Research Triangle Park. It is the fourth-largest nonprofit contract research organization in the United States. As for the park, it has

140 companies and employs almost forty thousand people, with combined annual salaries of over $1 billion. The research triangle is composed of Raleigh, Durham, and Chapel Hill, but its impact is felt throughout the state and the region. A decision made by a group in 1958 changed North Carolina's fortunes and future (Research Triangle Park, 2013).

America has always been the land of the opportunity built on a "can-do" spirit. Obstacle after obstacle has been tackled successfully by legions of men and women whose names we will never know. These people have shown heroics on the battlefield, in schools and colleges, in neighborhoods, in the streets, and in laboratories. Many of the things that we thought impossible are commonplace today. Sometimes the catalyst is one person or a small group who "catch fire" on an issue and just won't let go or take no for an answer. They just keep pushing and pushing to accomplish the task. The resilience of communities is built on the conviction of men and women who see possibilities in impossibility. These stories are inspirational, but most of all they provide an invaluable road map for community work: just do what you have to do. It is a new game in community work. People in communities must ask three critical questions to begin assessing their leadership capacity: Whom do we have, whom do we need, and how do we get whom we need?

A New Model for Leadership

The notion that leaders must be only elected, appointed, or anointed is no longer desirable or even practical. Communities need leaders who come through the ranks and from the rank and file. None of this happens by serendipity or by wishing it were so. Leadership occurs when individuals step up to the plate on important issues and when they are prepared to take on the difficult work.

The topic of leadership has become a field of academic inquiry and local practice. There are many for-profit companies, not-for-profit organizations, and educational institutions locally, nationally, and internationally that research, work, and train in the field of leadership. However, with all this important work on the study and practice of leadership, the critical and unanswered question is this: How can we spread it? The deliberate development of leaders has occurred in a relatively small percentage of Americans. Few ever get to attend a formal training program or have the opportunity to learn the skills and build the relationships needed to be effective leaders in our communities. At the same time, literally millions of individuals work with others in their neighborhood, local school, civic club, or religious organization to accomplish a task, develop a vision, or bring others together. These individuals are leaders but are not often asked to participate in larger community initiatives. It is time to build the leadership bench in communities with the wealth of people who already live there and invite them into the community conversation.

Building bench strength is a concept that coaches of team sports understand perfectly. Even though the most gifted players may start the game, others are prepared and ready to play at a moment's notice. Building bench strength in civic leadership is the most critical challenge facing our communities. The leadership called for today is found within a multitude of places and people. No longer is it necessary to think in terms of one leader or one group; communities are filled with people who want to make a difference where they live. As we think about the challenges facing the nation, none is more compelling than the need for more people to assume responsibility for leadership at all levels. For a community to achieve success, leadership must come from backyards and boardrooms.

One of the reasons we turn to traditional leaders is that they are there. Too many places and too many people have an impoverished view of leadership, one that sees only a few leaders. Years ago, a large project in an inner-city neighborhood had lost its original leaders. The project fell to a corporate group that had little knowledge or personal investment in the project. Because the project failed to move forward as quickly as it should have, it was suggested that some of the neighborhood leaders be included in the planning and implementation process. The group's response was, "There are no leaders in that neighborhood." There were people throughout the community who were ready to participate, solve problems, and yes, lead, but the established leaders thought otherwise. Their narrow view of leadership prevented the talents of far too many people from being fully used for the community.

The "usual suspects" in our community lives are critical to solving important community dilemmas, but we cannot solely rely on them no matter their talent. The "usual suspects" differ from community to community, but they likely include certain key businesspeople, well-known clergy, civic organization leaders, and representatives from local hospitals, schools, and nonprofit agencies. We need all those people, but we also need shop foremen, postal workers, stay-at-home parents, young people, senior citizens, public housing residents, and police officers, to name only a few. We have to look broader and deeper. But how and where?

In his work on paradigm shifts, Thomas Kuhn (1996) found that young scientists are the ones who have made many of the most significant discoveries. Applying this principle to community change suggests that involving young, new leaders with fresh ideas, enthusiasm, and new expertise can be greatly beneficial. The reality of today's challenges is that we can ill afford to exclude anyone's ideas from the community process. We have built too much of our lives and ways of working on the fault lines that divide us rather than on the ties that bind us. When the work is the focus in a community, not the personalities, vision supersedes individuals and ideas undercut stereotypes.

Moving from Hand-Wringing to Hand-Holding

There is no denying that times are tough. Communities have been hard hit by a changing global economy, shortfalls in revenue, and mounting social problems caused by years of disinvestment. In other words, it would be easy to give up and spend time and energy explaining why something can't be done, why a city or town is the way it is, and why the obstacles have stymied growth. But as the late U.S. Congresswoman Barbara Jordan explained, it is time for trading in the old for new ways of working: "We must exchange the philosophy of excuse—what I am is beyond my control—for the philosophy of responsibility." So how do we do this? How can we turn the tide? It is really pretty simple—just build the bench. To build the new leadership bench for communities, three realities must be front and center.

Leadership is no longer a pyramid but a plaza. As demographic diversity increases, there is a need to find more ways to involve and prepare people who are new to the community. This requires an understanding of cultural differences in authority, communication, and public participation traditions. Community leaders must be keenly aware of the barriers that have prevented participation among minority groups and remove them.

As cities become more important in the global matrix, local decision making really matters. Community members want and need a voice in the vision of the community. People want more control over the decisions affecting their lives, and they want more opportunities to interact with others on the wicked problems. This requires that people have the skills to work more effectively with others through partnerships, collaborations, and deliberative processes.

Finally, issues are more complex and interrelated. Community members need basic information and data, and they need to be able to connect the dots. So many of our social and economic challenges are interrelated that, in order to solve one, it is necessary to address another. This is both a message and a reality. This scenario requires leaders with new skills, new relationships, and new perspectives. A focused effort to "build the bench" can reinforce this new leadership. One agency or one sector or one well-intentioned person alone cannot address the systemic problems in our communities. Solutions will come, and only come, from a multilateral perspective, but that comes with a range of different opinions and the tensions that come with them. Leaders in all sectors must know how to manage conflict, how to communicate a broader agenda, and finally, how to convene groups and facilitate working together. Leadership must no longer be thought of solely in singular terms. The future of leadership development is "about the *we* not the *me*."

Potential Leaders Are All Around Us

The spark for change is sometimes hard to predict or pinpoint with certainty. Breakthrough leadership can come from elected leaders, corporations, organizations, or individuals—all of these are needed in order to build the bench for change.

Influential leaders are important every day on Main Street or Wall Street. In a letter written to chief executive officers to

encourage their civic involvement and participation in a corporate civic survey, the former chief executive officers of several
major corporations describe the challenge to the corporate community in this way: "Our leadership responsibility extends beyond
ensuring financial success and ethical business practices. We and
our associates are stewards of the cities and towns in which we
work, and we are responsible for fostering a strong sense of community throughout our enterprises—each and every day . . ."
(Case, Eskew, Nardelli, Pepper, and Chambers, 2012). America's
challenges require much more from corporations than attending
charity galas and supporting golf tournaments.

Real change comes from companies and organizations devot-
ing their time, collective talent, and resources to developing long-
term, sustainable action plans to improve their local communities
nationwide. Likewise, leaders from all sectors and from all socioeconomic groups help set the course for communities. They look
at the big picture—beyond their company, organization, or neighborhood. They act on the situation at hand.

Training literally hundreds of people over the years to participate more effectively in their communities has provided an invaluable opportunity to learn more about the leadership qualities that
communities need and have and how they foster more. Leaders
who respond well to disasters are important to have. However, it
is just as critical to have people who can anticipate problems and
opportunities and put systems in place to minimize disruption,
cost, or impact. In other words, would it be better to have a person
who anticipates or one who responds? Obviously, we need both,
but in all too many cases, leadership is just about responding. We
need leaders who understand investing in community, working
together, building on assets, creating avenues for community
deliberation, and managing the community process so that initiatives can move forward. Leaders can be the catalyst that pushes
ideas and progress forward—or backward. Rarely do things just
stay the same. A group of highly successful nonprofit, government, and civic leaders identified these characteristics of good
leaders: "saw the vision early on," "the glue that pulled it all
together," "was more of an evangelist than an administrator," "very
bright and very capable and very dedicated," and "people with

fire in their bellies." According to this group, they are traditional leaders, such as officeholders, business executives, and community foundation presidents, but they are also community leaders, such as neighborhood association members, knowledge holders, and trusted neighbors (Harwood Group, 1998, p. 27). What can a broad-based group like this bring to the community table? Lots. Try to make something really big happen and last without it. Leaders must have vision and persistence. They "see it" and "see it through" (Thorpe, 1998).

The Promise of Leadership

Communities cannot build a beautiful environment or create an optimum climate, but they can prepare and include people to enhance the prospects of the community and build a collective future.

Strong broad-based leadership is essential to community success. This leadership will change periodically, and the names of the people will surely change. That is the key to bench strength. Communities that rely on one industry, one family, or one perspective have missed the ideas, the resources, and the involvement of the "many." As communities consider their prospects for the future and who will carry the weight, they cannot look for one leader, *the* leader. Every community needs people "in the field"—backups, replacements, and new team members with new skills—to create a successful community. In baseball, you cannot just field a team of nine players. They get sick; they drop out; they move away. You must have reinforcements, trained and ready to play. As Yogi Berra would say, "You can observe a lot by watching" (1998, p. 95). If you watch successful communities, you'll see that they have strong leadership at all levels.

Success builds over time. Sure, a big employer might be landed or a bond issue approved, but success over the long haul requires sustained effort, organization of the work, and collective vision and action. Multiple stakeholders, the ability to build consensus around tough issues, and the courage to think and act strategically are what is needed. These leaders must have a passion for change but flexibility on how to get there. The leadership we need for communities is illustrated by the following cases. They represent political leadership, business leadership, thought leadership, and citizen leadership.

Elected Leaders Can Lead

When Mayor Joe Riley was elected to his tenth four-year term as mayor of Charleston, South Carolina, in 2011, he entered an elite group of local elected officials. One of the longest serving in modern history, Riley has the other unique characteristic of instilling the belief that citizens are the lifeblood of our local landscape. In an interview with Envision South Carolina, Riley was asked about his beliefs and his philosophy for leading one of America's midsized cities:

> In a democracy, you must be doing what the citizens' hearts would desire if fulfilled. You don't go off on a tangent because you have some personal idea that you believe would be great. You gotta believe that if this is accomplished, the citizens will rejoice in it. They will be fulfilled. Then you go about selling that. . . . Never, ever, ever take for granted the citizens that you're serving and always be asking yourself, "is this the right thing?" (April 23, 2013)

A city such as Charleston, South Carolina, is a perfect example of a leadership tipping point. For some communities, Riley's legacy might suggest a dynasty or the status quo. In Charleston, it suggests continuity in the midst of change and progress. When Riley took office in 1975, the City of Charleston was 16.7 square miles; today it is 90 square miles through annexation. Thirty years ago, the city was struggling with its downtown, balancing a military economy with a private one, and trying to create one community from a history of racial separation. Today it is a thriving example of what creative leadership can accomplish.

Perhaps Mayor Riley's greatest legacy will be his commitment to racial harmony and social progress. After his election in 1975, he worked aggressively to get more African Americans into leadership positions in the city and in the community. The turning points for communities often center on events, values, or opportunities. In the case of Charleston, Riley's leadership has led them to address three:

1. Commitment to affirmatively and aggressively open the government to everybody. (The practical application of this was to address racial challenges immediately and establish councils in neighborhoods throughout the city so that government could listen more effectively to citizens.)

2. Commitment to historic preservation.

3. Commitment to strategic planning and its follow-through.

Each of these strategies has been critical to Riley's leadership. Historic preservation in Charleston and Riley's innovative and dogged approach to preservation have saved untold priceless structures and restored the downtown as "the heart of the city." Using public-private partnerships as vehicles, Riley's efforts have pumped new life into areas throughout the city, with affordable housing, downtown development, and new amenities, such as a minor league baseball stadium and an aquarium. Under the mayor's watchful eye, the old has not been replaced by the new but rather complemented by it. Success in Charleston did not just happen. Not only did Riley have an eye for urban design and a love of history and architecture, but he also thought about how this project or that would maintain the integrity of the city (National Park Service, 2013).

Amid the ruins of a devastating hurricane in 1989, an economic downtown, and the loss of the naval base, Riley encouraged, prodded, and led the community to pursue strategies that made sense for Charleston. The economy is now stable and growing, the arts community is thriving, home to the world-famous Spoleto Festival, and the civic capital investments are visible and bringing thousands of tourists and residents to Charleston every day.

Is Charleston where it wants to be? Probably it is not "there" yet. Mayor Riley would likely agree. As he says, "If we are to build a great city and enhance the quality of life for every citizen, then we must realize that a great city is not great because of the size of its population. A city is great when it demands of itself excellence, protects its natural and built environment, and seeks a higher quality of life for every one of its citizens." That is why he has kept running . . . and kept winning.

Leaders Change the Conversation

Sometimes people come along at the right time or they make it the right time. Geoffrey Canada changed the way the entire nation thinks about preparing young people for productive futures by starting in one neighborhood, Harlem.

Geoffrey Canada is a pioneer in helping that neighborhood, and now many others in the nation understand why early and sustained investments in children are important and, most important, how this is done. The Harlem Children's Zone, where he has spent the last twenty years of his career serving as president since 1990, has identified one hundred blocks in Harlem and the ten thousand children who live there as their "Zone." Using a range of interventions, the project aims to create a safety net woven so tightly "that children cannot slip through it" (Bryant, 2011).

Working with children from babyhood through college, the model focuses on an integration of social, educational, and health development outcomes for children by investing in a range of programs that strengthen the family and the neighborhood. It is a bit early to determine conclusively that the program works, but the general consensus is that it does.

There are still doubters, but a ten-year evaluation of the Baby College, the program that works with parents to equip them with the skills they need to help their child get ready for school, showed that 81 percent of the parents who had completed the program said they read to their child five or more times a week. An evaluation of the Zone's two Promise Academy Charter Schools shows that the programs have demonstrated that they have reversed the black/white achievement gap in mathematics (Dobbie and Fryer, 2010). While the evaluation data will continue to show strengths and weaknesses and the model will be tweaked, Geoffrey Canada has changed the national conversation about ways to overcome poverty from individual programs to a holistic approach that starts early and stays the course.

Leaders Believe It Can Be Done

Saying that George McLean was just a good corporate citizen really misses the point. He was a community champion who never quit or let anyone else quit. Mark Twain once said, "Never pick a fight with people who buy ink by the barrel." This could well apply to George McLean, the owner and publisher of the *Northeast Mississippi Daily Journal* (formerly the *Tupelo Daily News*). He used his platform as the owner and publisher of the regional newspaper to promote and change the community in untold ways. He believed in giving voice to the community about its collective future.

Located in the northeast corner of Mississippi, away from the Delta region, away from the state's capital in Jackson, in fact away from most anything, Tupelo is a hundred miles from Birmingham and Memphis. A city of thirty-five thousand, Tupelo is far from isolated. It is home to a new Toyota Corolla manufacturing plant in nearby Blue Springs, and it has one of the last American outposts of Cooper Tire and Rubber. Its famed furniture industry, which took a hard hit from Chinese imports in the 1990s, is making a comeback. The region, including Lee County, was once the largest producer of upholstered furniture and the second-largest manufacturer of all furniture in the country. Today those numbers have shrunk, but furniture still figures into the economy. In addition, Lee County has the largest nonmetropolitan health care facility in the United States.

But what distinguishes Tupelo from any other small town trying to make ends meet is its renaissance story that began in the 1930s with the return of one of its native sons, George McLean. The city and surrounding areas were poor. Grisham describes it as "one of the poorest counties in the poorest state in the nation" (1999, p. 2). It had no natural resources, no advantageous location, and no real industry. In 1933 President Franklin Roosevelt himself brought some good news, making Tupelo the first city in the United States to be a Tennessee Valley Authority (TVA) community. The newly minted agency was charged with bringing not only electrical power to rural areas but also economic development efforts. Tupelo was a prime candidate for both.

The Tupelo story has many interrelated and fast-moving parts, but all of them contain the fingerprints of McLean and his supporters. They understood and promoted three important principles of renewal: working together, education, and community involvement. All three ideas point to the same concept: we are all in it together. According to local leader and businessperson Jack Reed Sr. (2003), it was not always smooth sailing. McLean's views were considered more liberal than the views of a significant number of people in Mississippi—so much so that there was a move to get a competing newspaper to come to Tupelo. Reed said that McLean quieted his critics. George McLean was bright and intelligent, and he also got things done. He "put his money where his mouth was," says Reed. He gained people's respect, if not always their full endorsement.

In order for progress to gain a footing, McLean knew that there had to be local people and organizations to spearhead the efforts. The first of these structures was the Northeast Mississippi Poultry Council, established in 1936 to shore up the efforts of poultry farmers in the region through marketing and development. Although this initial program led to limited success, it began a mind-set which led to organizing structures that coordinated singular efforts for greater impact. The real strokes of genius were the Rural Community Development Councils (RCDCs), created in the mid-1940s, and the Community Development Foundation created in 1948. These last two organizing structures allowed the region to move to a different level of work and working together (Grisham, 1999).

The RCDCs were opportunities and vehicles for every rural community in the seven-county area to take hold of its own development. Although TVA, a local college, and other firms provided technical assistance, the expectation was that the community itself would decide how it would develop, assess the improvements that were needed, and then determine its strengths. "The RCDCs were to think about all aspects of community development from education to farm management to housing" (McLean, 1946, quoted in Grisham, 1999, p. 95). By the 1950s, there were fifty-six councils, involving six thousand citizens, representing both black and white communities. The organizations developed projects that the newspaper would celebrate, and more and more people in the region began seeing their individual success tied to the collective success of their neighbors and their region.

The second big organization (or reorganization) was the elimination of the traditional chamber of commerce and the creation of the Community Development Foundation (CDF). McLean knew that business leadership was critical to Tupelo's success, but not just in the traditional way. McLean put forward the idea that economic development had to be linked to community development. In other words, the region needed an entity that focused on all aspects of the community and not only business development. Reed said that McLean knew that progress depended on a strong community. The idea made sense to people. The Community Development Foundation was formed in 1948 with 151 charter members, with the Rural Community Development Councils as its crown jewel. Communities and organizations began to look at Tupelo as a model for rural development. Former Secretary of Agriculture Orville Freeman said it was "the best program of rural development I have been exposed to anywhere around the country" (Grisham, 1999, p. 100). The CDF has met with tremendous success over the last fifty years. It has coordinated, spearheaded, and nurtured development in all areas. It has twelve hundred members and a standing in the region that allows it to represent the community on many fronts.

McLean and his wife founded a new community foundation, CREATE, Inc., which continues to support education and youth development. McLean himself gave $1 million to place reading aides in every first-grade classroom for a ten-year period. The investment paid off: scores on national standardized tests moved from the bottom quarter to the top half. Partnerships were built between and among local, regional, and federal organizations to promote all aspects of education, from literacy to job training to faculty development. L. D. Hancock, the founder of Hancock Fabrics, gave $3.5 million to establish an institute for teachers. At the time it was the largest gift to a public school system in U.S. history (Pittman, 1993).

Tupelo has done what others said could not be done. They have overcome obstacles, they have literally weathered storms, and they have bridged the fault lines of race and class in ways that other communities have not. The physical and demographic assets they lacked, they made up for with hard work, organization, and strong local leadership. McLean (cited in Collum, 2004) believed that people were a community's greatest resource and that each person had a responsibility to get involved. George McLean and other business leaders had a vision that a community working together could beat the odds. To achieve that goal, they took risks, worked hard to be inclusive, and had an expectation that everyone in the community would be a part of the future.

Organizations Taking the Long View

Local, regional, and national foundations are joining with a multitude of organizations in communities to support the common good through building leadership capacity. Realizing that building local capacity is absolutely critical to long-term community success, a state health foundation, Kansas Health Foundation, and a regional foundation, Northwest Area Foundation, identified local leadership development as a major conduit to address their primary focus areas of health and poverty, respectively.

Neighborhood, community, regional, and statewide leadership development initiatives have taken seriously the importance of both breadth and depth of leadership and capacity building. There are a whole cadre of traditional leadership groups, some sponsored by chambers of commerce or other independent organizations that serve an important function in identifying and grooming community members for larger roles in civic life.

These exemplary examples of direct investment in leadership development are instructive in understanding how other community organizations might broaden their reach and build more capacity for community members to influence their futures.

The Kansas Health Foundation, a health conversion foundation based in Wichita, is charged with improving the health of all Kansans. In the early days of its creation, the foundation spent time across the state on "listening tours" to get ideas and thoughts on ways to invest in a healthier Kansas. One persistent theme was the need to have more community members engaged in the long-term well-being of the community. Foundation board and staff members took this suggestion to heart and in 2007 invested $30 million over ten years to create the Kansas Leadership Center. Not satisfied with one or a few cities and towns with access to leadership development training, the Kansas Health Foundation decided to change the game. With the philosophy that leadership is an activity and not a person or position, the Leadership Center is offering training, coaching, and resources to cities, towns, nonprofit organizations, and religious organizations throughout the state. According to Steve Coen, president and chief executive officer of the Kansas Health Foundation, "the health and wellness challenges facing the State of Kansas—and the nation as a whole—are complex, dynamic, and oftentimes hotly debated. The foundation realized many years ago that to make significant progress toward the mission of improving the health of all Kansans, it needed to invest in creating an infrastructure that developed a generation of leaders unafraid of tackling the difficult topics and ready to rally people together to find solutions to the issues they face."

The primary reality that defines a community's success lies in its resiliency. According to the RAND Corporation, resiliency is defined as: "the sustained ability of a community to utilize available resources to respond to, withstand, and recover from adverse situations" (RAND Corporation, 2013). This requires that communities have within them people who can act on a situation not just react, bring others together to set a new agenda, and galvanize diverse stakeholders to take action. In other words, resilience needs leadership. The Kansas Leadership Center is one of only a handful of statewide initiatives that focus on big cities, small towns, and a wide array of organizations that have as their mission stronger, more vibrant communities.

....

The Northwest Area Foundation in St. Paul, Minnesota, launched a new initiative, Horizons, in 2004, with the goal of reducing poverty in small towns across the northwest region. Towns with under five thousand residents that had poverty rates of at least 10 percent or above were eligible to participate in the project. With an organizational mission to reduce poverty and achieve sustainable prosperity, the foundation worked with almost three hundred communities in eight states across the Northwest and Upper Plains in a dialogue, leadership, and capacity-building initiative to reduce poverty at the local level. Horizons was crafted to address a priority area of the foundation and build the long-term capacity in small towns across the Northwest to tackle this and other community issues—together. Because of the Horizons program, small Northwest towns and their members have had the chance to change the conversation in their communities. People in these towns participated in a multiphase community initiative that included visioning, community dialogue, leadership training, and action initiatives to improve or reduce poverty in small towns, rural, and reservation communities. The program tested whether community dialogue, skill-based leadership development, and an action agenda could make headway on the wicked problem of poverty.

Working with two national partners, Everyday Democracy's study circles and the Pew Partnership for Civic Change's LeadershipPlenty® program, and extension organizations in the participating states, the Horizons program partners conducted community discussions on poverty and used a train-the-trainer model to license more than one hundred community members to offer the nine-module, skill-based LeadershipPlenty program back in their home communities. Almost all of the towns lacked a formal leadership program and depended on the same group of volunteers to carry the load. According to the independent evaluators, the leadership changes as a result of this program have led to more civic initiatives, new elected leadership, and a collective sense of optimism about the future of the community (Morehouse and Stockhill, 2008). In a profile of the process and the program done by the Federal Reserve Bank of Minneapolis's *Dividends* newsletter, it cited the evaluation of three thousand LeadershipPlenty participants and the evidence that the curriculum was successful in strengthening the confidence and competence of new leaders. Coming into the program, most LeadershipPlenty participants, the article states, did not view themselves as community leaders. Post-program, participants showed statistically significant gains in knowledge and leadership skills on all survey items, including group development, community action, group problem solving, and community development (Hoelting, 2010).

According to Gary Cunningham (2013), vice president for programs at the Northwest Area Foundation, "Horizons certainly helped people across the region get engaged from a civic sense. The process brought issues to the fore. It created a sense of hope and built new knowledge and skills." More than one hundred thousand people, almost 30 percent of the populations of the participating communities, took part in the process. Since this was such a large and ambitious initiative, the foundation is still learning about its impact. One continuing area of inquiry is how to affect a global issue such as poverty on a local scale. Other learnings included the important role of intermediary partners, in this case the university extension unit; better and more effective ways to include and learn from communities of color and Native communities; and ways to integrate "best practices" on issues into a process.

More Leadership Is Better

Malcolm Gladwell's (2000) theory of the tipping point is a wonderful illustration of what effective collaborative leaders do: they tip the scales. The *tipping point* is the threshold at which ideas, trends, fashions, or even restaurants take hold. Leaders "tip" communities too. This notion of the tipping point—when diseases become epidemics or when a trend gets hot—helps us understand why the concentration of a broad and deep leadership team can make all the difference. The concentration of leaders in a community builds networks and relationships among citizens and organizations that are critical to making things happen.

Part of the challenge of reaching more broadly for new leaders is simply finding them and recruiting them. Often they do not appear on the traditional lists or frequent the same civic club. Sometimes we have to look closely to find the very people we need.

My grandmother was a quilter. The quilt she made for me decades ago was a bow-tie design, made from the dresses, shirts, and dusters that had belonged to me and to a host of relatives. I remember her saying that she was "piecing a quilt top" from variegated and seemingly dissimilar materials. Inventing a strategy for leadership, like quilting, is a complex process that takes an appreciation of resources that often can be overlooked. Quilts can be a metaphor for community leadership patterns. There is a place for the predominant design or color, but it wouldn't be a quilt without all the pieces (Pew Partnership for Civic Change, 2002).

It is essential that communities call forth the leadership possibilities that exist in people from all circumstances and experiences, reminding them and ourselves that we all are what John

Gardner calls "the responsibles," average citizens who work together across boundaries to make their communities better (Gardner, 1997). No longer is it desirable or even practical to build leadership pyramids—those closed, hierarchical structures based on traditional organizational charts. Rather, the task facing communities today is to build leadership plazas—open, inviting opportunities to put the whole community to work for the community. Leadership in its truest form is about connecting with others and ultimately catalyzing actions toward common interests. The pyramid model works from the assumption that leaders are few and followers are many. There are certainly times when decisions must be made by a few rather than the many, but the plaza model calls for a process of inclusion, decision making, and action that makes everyone "responsible."

CHAPTER EIGHT

| Inventing the Future

Ideas and inventions encompass things that are mechanical, social, and civic. Ultimately, inventions are about the future. As the inventor of the self-starter, Charles Kettering described the difference between most people and inventors, "Most people are interested in where they come from. Inventors are interested in where they are going" (1982, p. 72).

Civic inventions must ultimately improve a particular problem, the way we work, or where we are going. The idea is to straighten the road. Doing something better or more efficiently can often promise the same results, but only faster! The previous chapters focused on the experience and knowledge gained from the smart decisions of communities of varying sizes. The challenge is how to apply this strategic way of thinking in all communities—how to invent a way of making smart decisions that is "based on a leap of imagination" (Dyson, 2001, p. 2). All inventions start with a knowledge of what's already out there. They are built on the hard work and tested experience of others. The key to inventing is to assimilate the pieces and parts of the success and apply them to other situations in new ways.

Invention is a critical final piece to the smart communities' process. Ultimately, every community has to invent what will work for its circumstances. There are no cookie-cutter approaches to systemic change. The recipe for community success rests on the ability to invent the structure, process, and leadership to make long-term change.

Why Is Change So Important But So Hard to Manage?

Most people think change is what happens when our backs are against the wall and we have no choice. But actually change is the organic part of life that happens whether we like it or not. But even when we know that it is inevitable and we need to do it, often it takes a "near brink" experience to bring it to fruition. How many people do we know whose health diagnosis has triggered a lifestyle change? Communities can approach change and invention as business as usual or opportunity. Or they can be afraid, hold on tight to power and control, and refuse to accept new circumstances as reality.

It would seem that the logical way of working is to brace for the changes that surely are to come and have a process in place that manages, acts before reacting, and builds a collaborative process to discuss alternatives. The more likely scenario, however, is the "beat the devil syndrome." That is, individuals, organizations, and communities believe that the worst will not happen to them, they will be able to outrun the problems, or the ship will right itself with a few tweaks, budget cuts, and layoffs. Add to that the surprise shifts that come with personal life and community life and it is easy to understand why instigating change is so hard.

Even knowing what we know about change, it is still hard and unavoidable. Many places that were once bustling centers of commerce and population have found themselves on the wrong side of a changing economy, redirected transportation routes, and suburban housing patterns. Those hard hit are central cities, mature industrial or extraction places, and rural cities and hamlets. The nexus of their community identity has changed, moved away, or been forgotten in the crush of change. Unique places and cultural reminders have given way to the uniform, the convenient, and the conglomerate. This kind of typology could be applied to "mom and pop" grocery stores, downtown movie theatres, and the family farm to name only a few. In what is called cultural tourism or ecotourism, communities are finding that what seemed familiar, old-fashioned, or even an eyesore can provide a launch-pad for a new direction and identity for the community. The community and economic development field has seen a renaissance of these kinds of places and processes. Successful communities are inventing the future they want with what they have, the people they need, and a vision of the future that starts with imagination and possibility.

Innovation: Community Style

Innovation and its manifestations, technology and communication, have defined the global world. As work moved from a manufacturing economy to a knowledge economy, innovation was the link for those who had picked the right horse. It has become a buzzword and a cure-all for all economic and social ills. Everyone wants more of it: more innovative people, more innovative businesses, and more innovative communities. The assumption is that the first two—people and businesses—drive the third, communities. In reality, it is the reverse. Innovative communities actually drive the economy and quality-of-life investments in tandem. You can't have one without the other.

An innovative community is a place that builds the conditions for change. The concept of innovation as a public process has been overlooked or dismissed. As the Global Development Research Center (2013) in Kyoto, Japan, points out, "Innovation is about people. . . . An innovative community is not one founded to produce and distribute products invented by a single individual." Civic innovation is made possible by the collective civic inventiveness that is harvested and nurtured. Innovative communities create the conditions necessary to invent new civic practices and habits to design a new future. The creative economy is not just what we make or do, but it is how we work.

This is not to say that the literature on the innovative process is not helpful or applicable. However, if the traditional social entrepreneur model held true, communities would be destined to define their futures with only a few people located in the business park a few miles out of town. However, we know from years of research on what makes communities successful that it is more about how they work rather than the specific issues they address. Civic innovation is not about a person, place, or thing, but rather the mind-set and habits of how a community organizes and takes action on joint work. The word *innovation* has a number of formal definitions that explain the confusion. Per *Webster's*, it is defined as "the introduction of something new" or "a new idea, method, or device." For the community definition, it is important to go deeper. The Latin word for innovate is *innovatus*, meaning "to renew." That makes much more sense for successful communities as a process for renewing the foundational practice of deciding and working together—deliberation and collaboration.

Civic innovation allows communities to invent new ways of working and to reinvent their notion of the responsibilities and opportunities of their common vision. This is where the concepts of invention and entrepreneurship find some applicability. These concepts move beyond "things" to inventing a community that works in the new global environment, one that takes responsibility for what is and what might be, and one that improves the ability of a community to self-govern. The status quo is not the benchmark for success for entrepreneurs or inventors nor is it for civic innovators. Just ask Grand Rapids.

Grand Rapids—A City That Makes Things *and* Opportunities

With a population of slightly over two hundred thousand, Grand Rapids is the second-largest city in Michigan. A player in the automotive industry in the early part of the twentieth century, it is better known as the furniture capital for its early manufacturing footprint in that sector and now for office furniture with two of the largest companies, Steelcase and Herman Miller, located there. Grand Rapids is one of those places that has had many lives. In a state with distressed cities such as Detroit, Pontiac, and Flint, Grand Rapids is growing and diversifying in creative ways. The city has many physical amenities, but even more cultural and social ones that are contributing to its resilience. It is fortunate to have a number of other corporate headquarters including Wolverine, Meijer, and Amway, but it also has a growing medical research and development sector. Its "medical mile" has a range of hospitals, clinics, and research facilities run in part by Spectrum Health, western Michigan's largest employer. Despite a leg up in manufacturing and in health care, Grand Rapids has an upward trajectory because of the cooperation between the economic, community, and civic development sectors. Their success in becoming a sustainable city was not accidental; they worked for it—together.

One example of this "working together" mentality is the Grid70 Design Center championed by the chief executive officers of Amway, Meijer, Steelcase, Wolverine World Wide, and Pennant Health Alliance, who collectively have their companies' research-and-development efforts housed in the same location. The idea is to encourage collaboration and learning across sectors and to use and leverage proximity for creativity. While the sectors and the organizational structures are different, there is both industry-specific and general research going on. Since opening in 2010, the group has taken on more space and its first out-of-state partner, Process Automatic Concepts. According to Program Manager Kyle Los, "Whenever you think about collaboration, often there's the stigma of a brainstorming meeting where you spend four hours doing conversation about something you don't necessarily need. But it's through that casting of the net with people who all understand innovation and design and [are] beginning to hit a shelf process, that it really does speed along the creative process" (Morse, 2012; Nichols, 2013).

But the investments go far beyond economics. In the last decade Grand Rapids has built a new arena, invested $1 billion in health and health care–related facilities, and renovated the art museum and the Majestic Theatre, to name just a few things. In the summer of 2013, the 130,000-square-foot Downtown Market opened, which houses a range of culinary and local foods and what they call a "year-round hub of local food innovation, healthy-living education, and unique right-before-your-eyes preparation." The projection is that this facility alone will bring in half-a-million visitors per year and generate millions of dollars in new revenue for the city and surrounding areas. In addition to food, Grand Rapids is a growing stop on the beer tourism route. Touting the third-most-popular bar in the world, the city and surrounding area are home to breweries as well as the bars that sell their products. A real favorite for beer aficionados is the brewery located in a former funeral home (Noel, 2012). Add to all of this the new Michigan State College of Human Medicine and the downtown campus of Grand Valley State University, and the picture becomes clearer. Manufacturing is now the second-largest employer sector in the area; the first are health and education, which are tied.

In a time and a state that has taken one of the hardest economic hits in history, how has this medium-sized city defied the odds? There are wealthy and generous philanthropists there to be sure, but this is just the tip of the iceberg. In essence, the people from throughout the community worked together to create a vision of what was possible and then went to work. There were institutions that were critical to the process. A nonprofit business-leader group, Grand Action, joined with local development organizations and others to create a vision. This group was instrumental in raising the money for the Downtown Market. A now-sunsetted civic group called Delta Strategy was an early leader in bringing people together, benchmarking demographics and trends, and encouraging a dialogue about the present and the future.

Delta Strategy's annual report card, Community Counts, looked at a range of social and economic indicators pertaining to Grand Rapids and the region in general; it included comparisons to state averages to give a sense of how the city and region measured up. Grand Rapids shared many of the same challenges as other small-to-midsize cities in the Midwest. For example, there was a clear call to action around high school completion and the implications of that for the future workforce. Likewise, some social indicators needed real attention. The Delta Strategy numbers and comparisons were great benchmarks to begin some challenging but absolutely critical work. The efforts in Grand Rapids, however, didn't begin in 2007 but more than a decade earlier, when the Frey Foundation and others began to examine in detail what corporate-sponsored leadership could do. In *Taking Care of Civic Business*, efforts across cities that were mature industrial places such as Grand Rapids and Cleveland were profiled (Frey Foundation, 1993). A clear understanding existed even from that early time that civic work required the participation of the local business community. Delta Strategy, Leadership Grand Rapids, and other organizations filled out the palette by adding a broader group of people to the community conversation. While many upper-Midwest or Rust Belt cities have fallen on hard times,

Grand Rapids has held its own. Many cities would love to have just a fraction of the assets of Grand Rapids, but their greatest asset is themselves and their ability to work together. The transformation of the city is testament to that strategy.

Globalization Is Real . . . and Not a Surprise

When communities are faced with economic change, it can be difficult to let go of industries that were once economic, cultural, and social foundations. However, the fast-paced change in technology and manufacturing make the process to diversify employment sectors and determine new competitive strategies very time sensitive. As history has shown, this process is particularly counterintuitive when jobs are plentiful and industries are still producing; it is hard to channel energy and resources to new initiatives when the need is not apparent.

Cities of very different sizes, geographical locations, and key sectors all have been impacted by the global economy. Globalization has hit our economy, our communication system, and even our social lives by storm. No longer is there the assurance that American owners own a company with their name on it even if it is based in the United States. Not only are goods and products manufactured outside the United States that were once mainstays, such as textiles, shoes, and steel, but a huge services and information technology market is flourishing well beyond the borders of the United States. There is no better example of the impact of a declining sector than the Steel City itself, Pittsburgh.

Pittsburgh: Three Rivers and Nine Lives

Pittsburgh, Pennsylvania, provides an excellent example of the marriage of expectation and strategy when the economic forecast was dim and the current reality shaken. Prior to World War II, Pittsburgh was a grimy, smoky city. It was producing half of the country's steel, leading to so much air pollution that there were days when the streetlights had to be turned on during the daylight hours. Its air was toxic to breathe, and its rivers were polluted.

In the 1940s, however, local leaders saw the need to improve local environmental quality and regional transportation through a collaborative postwar planning committee. In 1944 the Allegheny Conference was officially established for those purposes. During the next few years, the conference advocated for city and county antipollution laws; clearing the skies attracted new businesses and heavily influenced the economic and physical revitalization of the city (Allegheny Conference on Community Development, 2013).

Because of the relationship-building work of the Allegheny Conference and other organizations, Pittsburgh was able to weather the shock of globalization when it first hit the U.S. manufacturing industry in the 1970s and 1980s. While the unthinkable had not yet occurred—the loss of over sixty-five thousand jobs in steel, an industry that had once comprised over 40 percent of the city's economy—Pittsburgh had begun the process of change and transformation and had already begun planting roots in the education, medicine, energy, and technology industries that form the backbone of its economy today.

Since then, the city has continued to pave the way in investing in its natural and environmental assets as a method for attracting diverse economic interests and enticing its talented youth and college graduates to stay there. For example, the banks of Pittsburgh's three rivers—the Allegheny, Monongahela, and Ohio—were once symbols of steel giants. In the past twenty years, however, public-private collaborations have worked to remediate brown fields, clean the water, and redevelop the city's waterfront, adding over twelve miles of recreational trails and acres of park space. The current master plan for private development along the Monongahela River echoes this environmental and civic sentiment, calling for alternative energy generation, storm and wastewater management, park space, trails, and river access.

Pittsburgh's strategy is working. In the fall of 2012, the Brookings Institution released a report stating that only three U.S. cities had hit economic recovery since the 2007–2009 Great Recession—Dallas, Knoxville, and Pittsburgh. This report marks tremendous progress for Pittsburgh, a city that lost over one hundred thousand jobs and 35 percent of its population in the three decades following World War II. The advancement that the city has made is, in part, because of its early commitment to collaboration in protecting and enhancing its natural assets.

More important, though, it is seeing the results in its job and population growth. Today Pittsburgh employs more people than it ever has, and no industry represents more than 23 percent of its economy. Investments in livability have positioned the city to attract and retain talented young professionals in flexible industries. Economic diversification and a culture of community collaboration will ensure that it weathers future economic storms—like that of globalization—with resilience.

Pittsburgh is a sterling example of a place that looks outward for information and inward for assets. It will always be the "steel" city in our minds, but now its identity goes far beyond one industry. Pittsburgh is the same place it always has been: a great place to live with many things to do, beautiful surroundings, world-class educational institutions, and an economy that has international dimensions and its future is bright.

The Maps Change

For the last century the U.S. auto industry has staked a claim to the upper Midwest and Northeast. Aside from the Michigan cities of Detroit, Flint, and Pontiac, well-known car cities ranged from Gary, Indiana, to Dayton, Ohio, to Rochester, New York, where cars were built, radiators were manufactured, and tires rolled off the assembly lines. Now Motown has been joined by a whole string of states that make Chevrolets and also Toyotas, Mercedes, and BMWs. Change came to the car industry and to the cities and towns in the Sunbelt that were ready.

Greenville-Spartanburg: The Transformation of a Manufacturing Footprint

From the end of the nineteenth century to the mid-twentieth century, Greenville-Spartanburg, South Carolina, was a region that realized that its largest sector, textiles, was slowly but surely declining even if it was known as the "Textile Center of the World." Investments in research could not erase the encroachment of lower-cost foreign goods. Most of the area's workers were employed in the nation's largest mills—weaving, spinning, and doffing. In addition to a few poultry plants and small farms, the community centered largely around one industry. But because of a few visionary leaders who foresaw the downturn of the American textile industry, a flexible, pro-business and pro-international culture, and a commitment to continuous workforce improvement, the region has been able to diversify and retool itself over the past sixty years.

Instead of waning with the disappearance of the mills, as did many other regions reliant on a single manufacturing industry, Upstate South Carolina has flourished as the fastest-growing region in the state, with an unemployment rate steadily below state and national averages and a stable, if not booming, economy.

This success is primarily attributable to continual and expanding investment by foreign companies in the area. The Upstate area houses over 240 international firms from 24 countries, including BMW, Michelin, Fluor, Samsung Networks America, Kyocera Mita, and Mitsubishi. Since 2000 over thirty international companies either have opened or have expanded their offices in Greenville County, representing foreign investments of over $1 billion and fifteen hundred new jobs (Greenville Area Development Corporation, 2013).

While today's international companies in the Upstate region represent a wide range of products and industries, the area first attracted companies from Germany, Switzerland, and Austria that produced parts for the textile mills. In the mid-1950s Roger Milliken, chief executive of Milliken and Company, saw the need to reduce costs by encouraging the European manufacturers that supplied the textile industry to move to South Carolina to be close to their customers. Richard Tukey, former executive director of the Spartanburg Chamber of Commerce, a "visionary who realized that opportunities had to be cultivated for a declining textile industry," got on board quickly to support the effort (Kanter, 2003, pp. 151–160).

Milliken and Tukey worked tirelessly to transform the Upstate region to be appealing to foreign executives, while capitalizing on South Carolina's pro-business attitude and its renowned worker-training program. Milliken collaborated with other business leaders in the area to improve the schools, airports, and the hospital and to form the Carolina Country Club for foreign companies (Kanter, 2003, p. 250). At the same time, Tukey went overseas to lure foreign investors and urged his allies in the state government to make the area more attractive to Europeans with business incentives and legal amendments. For example, he persuaded the South Carolina Legislature to amend alcohol laws so that Europeans could import wine more conveniently, and he started a German-style Oktoberfest. He also worked individually with potential investors, assisting them in site selection, legal issues, and the procurement of visas and housing.

The first foreign companies to expand to the Upstate were primarily German and German-speaking Austrian and Swiss producers of equipment for the textile mills. The cultural style of these people was to form roots and integrate into the local culture, learning English, becoming citizens, and establishing lives in South Carolina (Kanter, 1995, p. 246). Once the locals saw the economic benefit from the foreign companies as well as their commitment to the area, they were even more willing and eager to attract further foreign investment. In return, the Swiss and German leaders sent word back to Europe touting the benefits of South Carolina: the low cost of living, a skilled and inexpensive workforce, a culture of entrepreneurship, and inviting people. Since then, the industries of the area and the countries of foreign investment have expanded tremendously—to German automobiles, French tires, and Japanese technology—and investment continues to grow.

Currently Milliken and Tukey's efforts to make the Upstate more attractive to foreign investors have resulted in a small city with the cosmopolitan character of a much larger urban area—a metropolitan. There are numerous international restaurants, markets, grocery stores, shops, and associations, as well as many foreign language and English as a Second Language (ESL) programs. There are groups such as the Alliance Française de Piedmont, the Michelin French School, and the International Center of the Upstate—a nonprofit organization that offers assistance in finding schools and doctors and establishing life in the area, and hosts multicultural activities, events, and education programs (Greenville Area Development Corporation, 2013). Several local schools have International Baccalaureate Programs.

Today international businesses are attracted to the Upstate area for several reasons: a skilled, flexible, and inexpensive workforce; state and local incentives for foreign investment; a prime geographic location; and not least, a cultural environment that is welcoming and amenable to foreign manufacturing businesses. While the textile industry mostly has faded from the area, the Upstate continues to be a leader in manufacturing, constantly reinventing and upgrading itself with the higher education and skill levels demanded by these foreign companies. In addition, foreign investment has catalyzed investment by American companies. Success follows success. Greenville-Spartanburg has invented a very robust future because it imagined and acted on new strategies with new partners.

Sometimes You Have to Reboot

Hindsight is twenty-twenty. As we analyze cities that didn't make the turn with the new economy, we just assume that they did something wrong, kept doing the same things that had worked before, or turned a blind eye. Cumberland, Maryland, a place that could have said, "This is just too hard," did the opposite—they rebooted.

Cumberland, Maryland: A Path to Many Places

From a colonial frontier outpost ushering settlers through the Cumberland Narrows and into the Ohio Valley, through a bumpy postindustrial identity, to a thriving "right-sized" small city, the story of the City of Cumberland in western Maryland seems similar to other former industrial powerhouse cities in the Eastern United States. Yet it stands apart in its successful transition into an economic hub built on resilient manufacturing, railroads, tourism, and proximity to ample outdoor recreation opportunities throughout the Monongahela Valley that stretches from southwestern Pennsylvania into northeastern West Virginia.

General George Washington built the first outpost of the French and Indian War in Cumberland. As canals and railroads competed to dominate the commercial goods movement early in the nineteenth century, Cumberland became a prized destination for its links to western markets. The Baltimore and Ohio Railroad raced the Chesapeake and Ohio Canal to reach the city, beating it by years and arriving in 1842. Many early Americans immigrating west into the Ohio Valley passed through the town along the Cumberland Narrows, one of the few navigable passages through the Allegheny Mountains. Similar to many cities in the region, a robust manufacturing base built on access to natural resources during the Industrial Revolution began a slow slide after World War II and cut the town's population in half from 1950 to 2010. The town had fewer than 21,000 residents in the 2010 census.

Despite postindustrial economic transformation and significant population loss, Cumberland has remade its identity as a small, picturesque town with a diverse and solid economic base, attractive cost of living, and a housing market that continued to grow even throughout economic downturns. The city serves as a regional health care hub to western Maryland and northeastern West Virginia, with Western Maryland Health Systems employing over twenty-three hundred residents. A CSX Locomotive Facility located in the city provides over six hundred unionized positions and recently expanded its infrastructure to meet increased demand from freight trains traveling from Pittsburgh, Baltimore, and Washington, D.C.

The history, infrastructure, and presence of trains in the region have become a tourist draw for regional and distant visitors. The city lies at the terminus of the C&O Canal, which begins in Georgetown, D.C., and traverses an unbroken crushed stone canal towpath to Cumberland for 184 miles. The canal and its bordering path were designated as a national park after an eight-day hike organized by U.S. Supreme Court Justice William Douglas in 1954 to oppose a proposed freeway. This same path is part of the larger regional Great Allegheny Passage Trail, equidistant and accessible for over two hundred miles of traffic-free paths for residents of both Washington, D.C., and Pittsburgh. Cumberland is the third-largest town on the trail after these two metro areas and has adopted the image and moniker of a successful "trail town." The Western Maryland Scenic Railroad operates classic steam engines along a twenty-mile scenic route to Frostburg, Maryland, completing a loop that is completely traversable by cyclists via a successful rails-with-trails project.

In 2012 the National Association of Home Builders rated Cumberland's housing and economic conditions as improving, based on its role as a regional health care center and major employment opportunities in the area in manufacturing, construction, railroad maintenance, and higher education. Using the *Improving Markets Index*, it also considered Cumberland's growing arts scene, attractive and low-cost small-town vibrancy, and proximity to both large urban centers and tremendous outdoor recreational opportunities throughout the Valley and surrounding mountains. The unemployment rate in Cumberland was 10 percent lower than the rest of the country at the 2010 census, and it had a much higher percentage of owner-occupied units than the national average. The area has attracted both retirees and young families (National Association of Home Builders, 2012).

What elements have led to the successful revitalization of Cumberland since it began to experience rapid population loss in the mid-twentieth century? For one, the downtown business district led a highly participatory committee representative of multiple community stakeholders in an effort to create a pedestrian mall in response to the establishment of a suburban shopping mall in the 1970s. This coalition successfully garnered state and federal revitalization funds in conjunction with local leadership. Buoying on the early adoption of Smart Growth principles throughout the state, Cumberland's leadership has been working toward mixed-use downtown development, frequent programming on the pedestrian mall, and streetscape improvements for at least two decades. Another notably successful element of Cumberland's downtown revitalization was the hiring of two energetic, local retirees to become "downtown managers," ambassadors of sorts to build community support for government grants that stimulated private investments and interest.

While discussions over the fates of legacy, shrinking, transitioning, or sometimes dying cities continue across the United States, Cumberland's path provides a glimpse of one successful route based on location, bolstering base industries, and building on a relevant and living history. The town's proximity to urban centers becomes more important in a near future with the potential of high-speed regional transit options. New economic foundations such as health care have fulfilled a regional need, and the town has been lucky to retain a relevant and viable manufacturing base. Finally, a history of trains is respected and built on as trains become extremely relevant once again in this new century, based on an efficient regional goods movement sweeping the nation and plentiful existing rail infrastructure.

Final Thoughts

The centennial of the invention of flight occurred in 2003. There were celebrations of the evolution of flight from Dayton, to Kitty Hawk, to Washington, D.C. The remarkable thing about the Wright brothers' contraption was that it actually flew. The pieces worked in tandem. Applied separately, the leverage points discussed in this book will make a modicum of improvement. Applied together, they have enormous possibilities to change the future for communities. Like the Wright brothers' plane, the pieces fit together. In his book *To Conquer the Air*, James Tobin (2003) writes of the dogged determination of Wilbur Wright to solve the mysteries of flight. He believed with his heart and mind that airplane flight was possible. That kind of determination is what fuels this book. I believe that communities can be stronger and more successful for everyone if they make smart decisions. We need not accept the conditions and circumstances handed to us. Together we have the intellect, energy, and will to make our communities work better.

Experience has shown that no matter how much is spent on research, development, and urban experiments, the results fall short of the target. This is not to say that we don't need more strategic investments, but rather that we must keep reframing the questions and looking for the clues of success—all the while believing that cities are the key to our economic, social, and civic futures. Our imagination will catch up with our knowledge if we keep at it. Place is at the center of this imagination—what it can be, what it must preserve, how it must care and embrace, and how it can address centuries of inequities and injustice. This work is not a question of simply getting a better plan or shorter blocks or even more economic diversity—it is about creating places that work for everyone. Dana Meadows (2008, p. 180) said this, "The thing to do, when you don't know, is not bluff and not to freeze, but to learn." Learn we shall—from and with each other.

Smart communities are smart because they have made tough decisions, included more people in the process, built on their assets, and learned to adapt. Smart communities do what has to be done, no matter the obstacles. Those profiled in this book have demonstrated these qualities over and over. Am I an optimist about communities? You bet. What drives my belief in the framework for smart decisions is the even bigger possibilities. As Wilbur Wright once said to his sister, "My imagination pictures things more vividly than my eyes" (Tobin, 2003, p. 2). We must imagine our communities as places of hope, responsibility, and equality. This will make the possibilities for the future soar.

References

Adams, B., and Parr, J. *Boundary Crossers: Case Studies of How Ten of America's Metropolitan Regions Work.* College Park: Academy of Leadership Press, University of Maryland, 1997.

Advisory Council on Historic Preservation. "Heritage Tourism and the Federal Government: Summit I—Report of Proceedings." Washington, D.C.: ACHP, Nov. 14, 2002. [http://www.achp.gov/pubs-heritagetourismsummit.html]

Allegheny Conference on Community Development. Pittsburgh, Pennsylvania, 2013. [http://www.alleghenyconference.org/ConferenceHistory.php].

American Society of Civil Engineers. *Report Card for America's Infrastructure.* Reston, Va.: American Society of Civil Engineers, 2013.

American Society of Landscape Architects. 2013. Awards of Excellence. [http://www.asla-ncc.org/awards-2/2013-awards-2/].

Anderson, L. A., Brown-Graham, A., and Lobenhofer, J. "Public Leadership of a Downtown Revitalization." *Popular Government,* Spring/Summer 2007. (Publication of the Chapel Hill Institute of Government, University of North Carolina.)

Anderson, L. C. "Promoting Civil and Human Rights Worldwide Through Education: The Birmingham Civil Rights Institute." In J. Hicks, S. Azshar, and C. Lewis (eds.), *Museums in a Global Context.* Washington, D.C.: AAM Press, 2013.

Ann Arbor SPARK. *Annual Report,* 2006. [http://www.annarborusa.org/succeed-here/annual-report].

Annie E. Casey Foundation. *Safety and Justice for Communities.* Baltimore: Annie E. Casey Foundation, 1999.

Annie E. Casey Foundation. *KIDS COUNT®.* Baltimore: Annie E. Casey Foundation, 2013. [http://datacenter.kidscount.org/publications/databook/2013].

Armbruster, A. "The Interstate Highway System: Its Development, and Its Effects on the American Spatial, Economic, and Cultural

Landscape." Unpublished paper, Eastern Michigan University, April 5, 2005.

Asheville Revitalization Commission. "A Revitalized Downtown." Asheville, N.C.: Asheville Revitalization Commission, August 1978.

Atkinson, R. D., and Correa, D. K. *The 2007 State New Economy Index.* Washington, D.C.: The Information Technology and Innovation Foundation.

Auter, D. H., Dorn, D., and Hanson, G. H. "The China Syndrome: Local Labor Markets and Import Competition in the United States." Working paper, National Bureau of Economic Research, May 2012.

Balfanz, R., and Legters, N. *Statistics Underestimate Dropout Numbers.* Cambridge, Mass.: Harvard Graduate School of Education, 2004.

Barber, B. 1988. *The Conquest of Politics: Liberal Philosophy in Democratic Times.* Princeton, N.J.: Princeton University Press.

Barrett, M. "The Balancing Act." *Asheville Citizen-Times*, Jan. 28, 2003, p. A14.

Bat Conservation International. "Congress Avenue Bridge." [http://www.batcon.org/index.php/get-involved/visit-a-bat-location/congress-avenue-bridge.html].

Beck, R. "The Ordeal of Immigration in Wausau." *Atlantic Monthly*, April 1994, *273*(4), 84–97.

Berra, Y. *The Yogi Book.* New York: Workman, 1998.

Best Management Practices Center of Excellence. "Best Practice: Greenways." Chattanooga, Tenn.: City of Chattanooga, 2007. [http://www.bmpcoe.org/bestpractices/internal/chatt/chatt_3.html].

Birmingham Civil Rights Institute. "Annual Report: Birmingham, AL, 2002." *Vision*, 2002, *3*(4) (Tenth Anniversary Commemorative Issue).

Blackwell, A. "Defining Community Building." Oakland, Calif.: National Community Building Network, 2005.

Blakely, E. J., and Leigh, N. G. *Planning Local Economic Development.* (4th Ed.). Thousand Oaks, Calif.: Sage, 2010.

Brennan, M. "Inspiring Projects—Submit Yours by June 30th!" June 19, 2013. [http://hackforchange.org/blog/inspiringprojects-submit-yours-june30th].

Brodie, M. J. Speech given in Japan, 1997. Used by permission.

Brown, T. *Change by Design.* New York: HarperCollins, 2009.

Brugmann, J. *Welcome to the Urban Revolution.* New York: Bloomsbury Press, 2009.

Bryant, A. "To Stay Great, Never Forget Your Basics." *New York Times,*
    Dec. 18, 2011, B42.

Bryson, J. M., and Crosby, B. C. *Leadership for the Common Good: Tackling
    Public Problems in a Shared-Power World.* San Francisco: Jossey-Bass,
    1992.

Burt, M. R. *Why Should We Invest in Adolescents?* Washington, D.C.:
    Urban Institute, 1998.

Carcasson, M., and Sprain, L. "Key Aspects of the Deliberative
    Democracy Movement." Fort Collins: Colorado State University,
    Center for Public Deliberation, 2010. [http://www.cpd.colostate
    .edu/keyaspects.pdf].

Case, S., Eskew, M., Nardelli, B., Pepper, J., and Chambers, R. "An
    Open Letter from 5 CEOs." National Conference on Citizenship,
    Philadelphia, July 24, 2012.

Chaskin, R. J. *Defining Community Capacity: A Framework and Implications
    from a Comprehensive Community Initiative.* Chicago: Chapin Hall
    Center for Children, University of Chicago, 1999.

Chaskin, R. J., Brown, P., Venkatesh, S., and Vidal, A. *Building
    Community Capacity.* New York: Aldine de Grayter, 2001.

Chrislip, D. D., and Larson, C. E. *Collaborative Leadership: How Citizens
    and Civic Leaders Make a Difference.* San Francisco: Jossey-Bass,
    1994.

City of Jefferson, Texas. 2013. [http://www.jefferson-texas.com
    /history/].

City of Lake Oswego. Capital Improvement Plan FY 2013/14–2017/18.
    City of Lake Oswego, Oregon, June 4, 2013. [http://www
    .ci.oswego.or.us/sites/default/files/fileattachments/publicworks
    /webpage/11842/cip-adoped-2013–14–0.pdf].

City of Portland Bureau of Planning and Sustainability. *Airport Futures:
    Charting a Course for PDX.* November 26, 2008. [http://www
    .pdxairportfutures.com/Documents.aspx].

Clarion Associates. *The Economic Power of Heritage and Place.* Denver:
    Colorado Historical Foundation, October 2011. [http://www
    .historycolorado.org/sites/default/files/files/OAHP/crforms
    _edumat/pdfs/1620_EconomicBenefitsReport.pdf].

Cleveland State University. "Estimates of the Economic Importance of
    the Ohio Historic Preservation Tax Credit Program on the State
    of Ohio." Cleveland: The Great Lakes Environmental Finance
    Center, Maxine Goodman Levin College of Urban Affairs,
    Cleveland State University, May 11, 2011.

Coates, J. F. "Impacts We Will Be Assessing in the Twenty-First
    Century." *Impact Assessment Bulletin,* 1991, *9*(4), 8–25.

Collins, J. *Good to Great*. New York: HarperBusiness, 2001.

Collins, R., Waters, E. B., and Dotson, B. A. *America's Downtowns: Growth, Politics and Preservation*. Washington, D.C.: Preservation Press, 1991.

Collum, D. D. "The Tupelo Miracle." [http://sojo.net/magazine /2004/10/tupelo-miracle].

Council on Foundations. *When Community Foundations and Private and Corporate Funders Collaborate*. Washington, D.C.: Council on Foundations, 1995.

Cunningham, G. Personal communication, July 16, 2013.

Deitz, R., and Orr, J. "A Leaner, More Skilled U.S. Manufacturing Workforce." Federal Reserve Bank of New York. *Current Issues in Economics and Finance*, February/March 2006, *12*(2).

Delgado, G. *Beyond the Politics of Place: New Directions in Community Organizing in the 1990s*. Oakland, Calif.: Applied Research Center, 1997.

Dewar, T., Dodson, D., Paget, V., and Roberts, R. *Just Call It Effective*. Richmond, Va.: University of Richmond, Pew Partnership for Civic Change, 1998.

Ditmer, J. "Preservation Becomes Profitable." *Denver Post*, Feb. 11, 2001, p. G2.

Dobbie, W., and Fryer, R. G., Jr. "Are High Quality Schools Enough to Close the Achievement Gap? Evidence from a Social Experiment in Harlem." Working paper no. 15473, *NBER Digest*, National Bureau of Economic Research, March 2010.

Dowdall, E., and Warner, S. *Shuttered Public Schools: The Struggle to Bring Old Buildings to Life*. Philadelphia: The Pew Charitable Trusts, February 11, 2013.

Dusack, M. "Twenty-Five Years of Jacksonville Community Council Inc. Makes a Difference." *Neighborhoods*, July–Aug. 2000, pp. 33–35.

Dyson, J. *A History of Great Inventions*. New York: Carroll & Graf, 2001.

Emery, M., and Flora, C. "Spiraling Up: Mapping Community Transformation with Community Capitals Framework." *Community Development: Journal of the Community Development Society*, April 2006, *37*(1), 19–35.

Envision South Carolina. April 23, 2013. Interview with Joe Riley. [http://envisionsc.org/interviews.php].

Erickson, A. "The Big Fix: Why Can't We Just Convert Vacant Buildings into Housing for the Homeless?" *The Atlantic Cities*, June 28, 2012. [http://www.theatlanticcities.com/politics/2012 /06/why-its-not-easy-convert-vacant-buildings-housing-homeless /2345].

Florida, R. *The Rise of the Creative Class: And How It's Transforming Work, Leisure, Community, and Everyday Life.* New York: Basic Books, 2002.

Forker, J. "The Future That Never Was." *Worcester Telegram & Gazette,* July 28, 2013. [www.telegram.com/article].

Freedman, P. *What Makes a Solution?* Charlottesville, Va.: Pew Partnership for Civic Change, 2003.

Frenchman, D., and Lane, J. S. "Assessment of Preservation and Development in the Lowell National Historic Park at Its 30-Year Anniversary." Discussion white paper, 2008.

Frey Foundation. *Taking Care of Civic Business.* Grand Rapids, Mich.: Frey Foundation, 1993.

Friedman, T. *The Lexus and the Olive Tree.* New York: Anchor Books, 2000.

Friedman, T. *The World Is Flat.* New York: Farrar, Straus and Giroux, 2005.

Gallagher, L. *The End of the Suburbs.* New York: Portfolio/Penguin, 2013.

Gardner, J. W. *On Leadership.* New York: Free Press, 1990.

Gardner, J. W. "You Are the Responsibles." *Civic Partners: The Search for Solutions.* Charlottesville, Va.: Pew Partnership for Civic Change, 1997, pp. 3–7.

Garvin, A. *The American City: What Works, What Doesn't.* New York: McGraw-Hill, 1996.

Gastil, J. 2012. [http://www.democracyfund.org/blog/entry/guest-post -the-oregon-citizens-initiative-review].

Gates, V. "The Birmingham Civil Rights Institute." *Alabama Heritage,* Fall 2002, pp. 17–25.

Gladwell, M. *The Tipping Point.* New York: Little, Brown, 2000.

Global Development Research Center. "Innovative Communities." 2013. [http://gdrc.org/susdev/inn-comm/index.html].

Gray, B. *Collaborating: Finding Common Ground on Multiparty Problems.* San Francisco: Jossey-Bass, 1989.

Green Design Atlas. 2013. [www.portlandoregon.gov/greenatlas/].

Green, G. P., and Haines, A. *Asset Building and Community Development.* Thousand Oaks, Calif.: Sage, 2002.

Greenville Area Development Corporation (GADC). Greenville, South Carolina, 2013. [http://www.greenvilleeconomicdevelopment .com/international.php].

Grisham, V. L., Jr. *Tupelo: Evolution of a Community.* Dayton, Ohio: Kettering Foundation Press, 1999.

Grogan, P. S., and Proscio, T. *Comeback Cities.* Boulder, Colo.: Westview Press, 2000.

Gutierrez-Montes, I. *Healthy Communities Equals Healthy Ecosystems? Evolution(and Breakdown) of a Participatory Ecological Research Project Towards a Community Natural Resource Management Process, San Miguel Chimalapa (Mexico).* Unpublished doctoral dissertation, Iowa State University, Ames, Iowa (cited in Emery and Flora, 2006).

Ha, S. *An Economic Benefit Study to Establish an Asheville Downtown Business Improvement District.* Asheville, N.C.: City of Asheville, 2011.

Hack for Change. 2013. [http://www.hackforchange.org/].

Halpern, R. *Rebuilding the Inner City.* New York: Columbia University Press, 1995.

Hammer, J. "Applying Triple Bottom Line Analysis to Development Decisions in the Portland Metro Region: Findings and Implications of Focus Groups with Municipal and County Officials." Portland, Oreg.: College of Urban and Public Affairs, Portland State University, September 2010. [http://www.pdx.edu/sites/www.pdx.edu.cupa/files/TBL_Lens_to_Development_2010.pdf].

Hammer, J., Babcock, J., and Moosbrugger, K. *TBL Casebook: Putting Concepts into Practice: Triple Bottom Line Economic Development.* U.S. Economic Development Administration, Technical Report Award Number 99–07–13871, September 2012. [http://www.tbltool.org/files/CUPA_Casebook.pdf].

Hammer, Siler, George Associates. *Lower Downtown Economic Impact of Historic District Designation.* Denver: Hammer, Siler, George Associates, 1990.

Harmon, K. M. "Moving Toward Urban Sustainability: A Comparison of the Development of Sustainability Indicators in Seattle and Minneapolis." In L. C. Herberle and S. M. Opp (eds.), *Local Sustainable Urban Development in a Globalized World.* Burlington, Vt.: Ashgate Publishing, 2008.

Harwood Group. *Planned Serendipity.* Charlottesville, Va.: Pew Partnership for Civic Change, 1998.

Henton, D., Melville, J., and Walesh, K. *Grassroots Leaders for a New Economy: How Civic Entrepreneurs Are Building Prosperous Communities.* San Francisco: Jossey-Bass, 1997.

Hibbard, M., Lurie, S., and Morrison, T. H. "Healthy Economies, Health Environments: Multifunctionality and the Natural Resources Economy." Rural Futures Lab, Foundation paper, no. 5, April 2012. [http://www.ruralfutureslab.org/NNRI.pdf].

Himmelman, A. T. "Communities Working Collaboratively for Change." In M. Herrman (ed.), *Resolving Conflict: Strategies for Local Government.* Washington, D.C.: International City/County Management Association, 1994, pp. 24–47.

Historic Denver. 2011. [www.historicdenver.org/get-involved /candidate-survey/].

Hoelting, J. "Horizons Program Mobilizes Community to Address Rural Poverty." *Community Dividends.* Federal Reserve Bank of Minneapolis, April 1, 2010.

Hoyt, L., and Leroux, A. *Voices from Forgotten Cities.* Berkeley, Calif.: PolicyLink, 2007.

Hunter, E. C., and McGill, K. Y. *Small Voices, Big Songs.* Asheville, N.C.: HandMade in America, 1999.

Huspeni, D. "Zeller Buys Guaranty Bank Building in LoDo." *Denver Business Journal,* April 1, 2013. [http://www.bizjournals.com /denver/blog/real_deals/2013/04/zeller-buys-guaranty-bank -building-in.html].

Isaacs, W. *Dialogue and the Art of Thinking Together.* New York: Doubleday, 1999.

Istrate, E., and Nadeau, C. A. *Metro Monitoring Report: Slowdown, Recovery, and Interdependence.* Washington, D.C.: Brookings Institution, 2012.

Jacobs, J. *The Death and Life of Great American Cities.* New York: Vintage Books, 1961.

Joint Fiscal Committee. Minutes of the Vermont Legislature, Sept. 26, 2011. [www.leg.state.vt.us/jfo/jfz/2011...2011_09_26_JFC _Minutes.pdf].

Kanter, R. M. *World Class: Thriving Locally in the Global Economy.* New York: Simon & Schuster, 1995.

Kanter, R. M. "Global Competitiveness Revisited." *The Washington Quarterly,* Spring 1999.

Kanter R. M. "Kaleidoscope Thinking." *Executive Excellence,* July 2000, p. 15.

Kanter, R. M. "Thriving Locally in the Global Economy." *Harvard Business Review,* August 2003, pp. 151–160.

Kanter, R. M. "The Enduring Skills of Change Leaders." *NHRD Journal,* 2007, *1,* 53–59.

Kettering, C. F. *Kettering Digest.* Dayton, Ohio: Reflections Press, 1982.

Kettering Foundation. *Communities That Work.* Dayton, Ohio: Kettering Foundation, 1998.

Kettering Foundation. *Making Choices Together: The Power of Public Deliberation.* Dayton, Ohio: Kettering Foundation, June 2002.

Klaassen, I. "The Future of European Towns." *Urban Studies*, 1993, *24*, 251–257.

Klein, W. R., Benson, V. L., Anderson, J., and Herr, J. B. "Visions of Things to Come." *Planning*, 1993, *59*(5), 10–19.

Knobloch, K. R., Gastil, J., Richards, R., and Feller, T. *"Evaluation Report on the 2012 Citizens' Initiative Reviews for the Oregon CIR Commission.* State College, Penn.: Pennsylvania State University, 2013. [http://www.la1.psv.edu/cas/jgastil/CIR/ReportToCIR Commission2012.pdf].

Koerner, B. J. "Cities That Work." *U.S. News and World Report*, June 8, 1998, pp. 30–31.

Kolko, J. *Wicked Problems: Problems Worth Solving.* Austin, Tex.: Austin Center for Design, March 2012. e-book. [https://wicked problems.com/1_wicked_problems.php].

Kotkin, J. "America's Fastest Growing Cities." June 18, 2013. [www .forbes.com/sites/joelkotkin/2013/06/18/America's_fastest _growing_cities]

Kresl, P. K. "The Determinants of Urban Competitiveness: A Survey." In P. K. Kresl and G. Gappert (eds.), *North American Cities and the Global Economy.* Thousand Oaks, Calif.: Sage, 1995.

Kretzmann, J., and McKnight, J. *Building Communities from the Inside Out: A Path Toward Finding and Mobilizing a Community's Assets.* Evanston, Ill.: Center for Urban Affairs and Policy Research, Northwestern University, 1993.

Kuhn, T. *The Structure of Scientific Revolutions.* (3rd ed.). Chicago: University of Chicago Press, 1996.

Larsen, L. H. *The Urban South: A History.* Lexington: University Press of Kentucky, 1990.

Lisheron, M., and Bishop, B. "Austin's Fast-Growing Immigrant Community Is Source of Wealth." *Austin American-Statesman*, June 9, 2002. [http://www.statesman.com/specialreports/content /specialreports/citiesofideas/0609immigration.html].

Logan, J. R., and Rabrenovic, G. "Neighborhood Associations: Their Issues, Their Allies, and Their Opponents." *Urban Affairs Quarterly*, 1990, *26*(1), 68–94.

Lowell National Historical Park. 2013. [http://www.nps.gov/lowe /loweweb/Lowell_History/rebirth.html].

Lucy, W. *Downtown Revitalization: Charlottesville, Virginia.* Charlottesville: City of Charlottesville, Virginia, 2002.

Luke, J. S. *Catalytic Leadership: Strategies for an Interconnected World.* San Francisco: Jossey-Bass, 1998.

MacDonald, J. M., and Sampson, R. J. "Don't Shut the Golden Door." *New York Times*, June 19, 2012, p. A29.

Maclaren, V. W. "Urban Sustainability Reporting." *Journal of the American Planning Association*, 2004, *62*(2), 184–203.

MacMahon, E. T. "From Skid Row to LoDo: Historic Preservation's Role in Denver's Revitalization." Urban Land Institute online, 2012. [http://urbanland.uli.org/Articles/2012/Oct /McMahanLoDo].

Markusen, A., and Gadwa, A. *Creative Placemaking*. Washington, D.C.: Mayor's Institute on City Design, 2010. [http://arts.gov/pub /pubDesign.php].

Mathews, D. *Politics for People: Finding a Responsible Voice*. (2nd ed.). Urbana: University of Illinois Press, 1999.

Mayo, M. Personal communication, 2003.

McCoy, M., and Scully, P. "Deliberative Dialogue to Expand Civic Engagement: What Kind of Talk Does Democracy Need?" *National Civic Review*, Summer 2002, *91*(2).

McGinn, M. Mayor's website, City of Seattle, Washington, March 6, 2013. [http://mayormcginn.seattle.gov/setting-a-new-goal -for-seattles-stormwater-management].

McKnight, J., and Block, P. *The Abundant Community: Awakening the Power of Families and Neighborhoods*. San Francisco: Berrett-Koehler, 2010.

McNulty, R. H. "Quality of Life and Amenities as Urban Investments." In H. Cisneros (ed.), *Interwoven Destinies: Cities and the Nation*. New York: Norton, 1993.

Meadows, D. *Thinking in Systems: A Primer*. D. Wright (ed.). White River Junction, Vt.: Chelsea Green Publishing, 2008, p. 105.

Medoff, P., and Sklar, H. *Streets of Hope: The Rise and Fall of an Urban Neighborhood*. Cambridge, Mass.: South End Press, 1994.

Michigan Historic Preservation Network. "Investing in Michigan's Future: The Economic Benefits of Historic Preservation." 2002. [http://www.mhpn.org].

Monkkonen, E. *America Becomes Urban: The Development of U.S. Cities and Towns, 1780–1980*. Berkeley: University of California Press, 1988.

Morehouse D. L., and Stockdill, S. H. *Northwest Area Foundation Horizons Phase II Program: Final External Evaluation Report*. Northwest Area Foundation, September 2008. [http://extension .ag.uidaho.edu/horizons/reports/H2%20Final%20Version%20 101508%20revised.pdf].

Morrison, C. "Housing Prices Soar." *Asheville Citizen-Times*, Jan. 27, 2003, pp. A1, A5.

Morse, S. W. *Building Collaborative Communities*. Charlottesville, Va.: Pew Partnership for Civic Change, 1996.

Morse, S. W. *Smart Communities: How Citizens and Local Leaders Can Use Strategic Thinking to Build a Brighter Future*. San Francisco: Jossey-Bass, 2004.

Morse, S. W. "Innovation as Civic Work. Unpublished paper prepared for the Kettering Foundation, Dayton, Ohio, 2011.

Morse, S. W. "Help Wanted: Innovative Leadership for the Community." *Leader to Leader*, Fall 2012(*66*), pp. 21–25.

Mossberger, K., Tolbert, C. J., and McNeal, R. S. *Digital Citizenship: The Internet, Society, and Participation*. Cambridge, Mass.: MIT Press, 2008.

National Association of Home Builders. "Improving Markets Index: Cumberland, MD-WV USA." [http://eyeonhousing.wordpress.com/tag/economic-recovery-in-cumberland/Aug212012].

National Park Service, U.S. Department of the Interior. "Chesapeake & Ohio Canal National Historical Park: Associate Justice William O. Douglas." 2013. [http://www.nps.gov/choh/historyculture/associatejusticewilliamodouglas.htm].

National Trust for Historic Preservation. 2013. [http://www.nationaltrust.org].

Nichols, M. "Grid70 Design Hub Expands Downtown." *Grand Rapids Business Journal*, April 11, 2013. [www.grbj.com/articles/76584-videos-grid70-designer-hub-expands-downtown].

Noel, J. "A Genuinely 'Grand' Spot for Beers." *Chicago Tribune*, August 12, 2012. [www.articles.chicagotribune.com/2012-08-12/travel/@t-travel-0812-grand-rapids-20120812_1_leinenkugel-beer-city-usa-darker-beers].

Norrell, R. J. *The Alabama Story*. Tuscaloosa, Al.: Yellowhammer Press, 1993.

North, D. *Understanding the Process of Change*. Princeton, N.J.: Princeton University Press, 2005.

Obama, B. "Transparency and Open Government." Memorandum, The White House, Washington, D.C., 2009. [http://www.whitehouse.gov/the_press_office/TransparencyandOpenGovernment].

Oldenburg, R. *The Great Good Place: Cafes, Coffee Shops, Community Centers, Beauty Parlors, General Stores, Bars, Hangouts, and How They Get You Through the Day*. New York: Paragon House, 1989.

O'Mara, M. P. *Cities of Knowledge: Cold War Science and the Search for the New Silicon Valley.* Princeton, N.J.: Princeton University Press, 2005.

O'Neill, T. Personal communication, July 2013.

Pahlka, J. *Coding a Better Government.* TED Talk video. 2012. [http:// blog.ted.com/2012/02/29/possum-problems-and-building -better-government-jennifer-pahlka-at-ted2012].

Pan, R. J., Littlefield, D., Valladolid, S., Tapping, P. J., and West, D. C. "Building Healthier Communities for Children and Families: Applying Asset-Based Community Development to Community Pediatrics." *Pediatrics,* April 2005, *155*(4).

Peirce, N. R., and Guskind, R. *Breakthrough.* New Brunswick, N.J.: Center for Urban Policy Research, Rutgers University, 1993.

Peña, F. Personal interview, 2003.

Pew Partnership for Civic Change. *In It for the Long Haul: Community Partnerships Making a Difference.* Charlottesville, Va.: University of Richmond, 2001.

Pew Partnership for Civic Change. *Crafting a New Design for Civic Leadership.* Charlottesville, Va.: University of Richmond, 2002.

Pew Partnership for Civic Change. *What Will It Take? Making Headway on Our Most Wrenching Problems.* Charlottesville, Va.: University of Richmond, 2003.

Pew Research Center. "For Nearly Half of America, Grass Is Greener Somewhere Else: Denver Tops List of Favorite Cities." Washington, D.C.: Pew Research Center, January 29, 2009.

Pittman, D. *Tupelo: Vision at the Crossroads.* Tupelo, Miss.: CREATE, Inc., 1993.

Porter, M. "The Competitive Advantage of the Inner City." *Harvard Business Review,* May–June 1995, *73*(3), 55–71.

Porter, M. "Location, Competition, and Economic Development: Local Clusters in a Global Economy." *Economic Development Quarterly,* 2000, *14*(1), 15–34.

Portney, K. E. *Taking Sustainable Cities Seriously.* Cambridge, Mass.: MIT Press, 2003.

Potter, J. G. *Great American Railroad Stations.* New York: Wiley, 1996.

Pretty, J. *A Living Land.* London: Earthscan, 1998.

Price, W. "Architectural Review Board Handbook." Richmond, Va.: Preservation Alliance of Virginia, 2005. [http://www .vapreservation.org].

Putnam, R. *Bowling Alone: The Collapse and Revival of American Community.* New York: Simon & Schuster, 2000.

Rabinovitz, F. *City Politics and Planning*. Rockaway Beach, N.Y.: Lieber-Atherton, 1969.

Race and Social Justice Initiative (RSJI). 2012. [http://www.seattle.gov/rsji/].

Race and Social Justice Initiative (RSJI). 2013. [http://www.seattle.gov/rsji/].

RAND Corporation. "Community Resilience." Santa Monica, California, 2013. [www.rand.org/topics/community-resilience.html].

Read, A. "Asset-Based Economic Development and Building Sustainable Rural Communities, Part 3: Existing Infrastructure, Historic and Cultural Resources." Washington, D.C.: ICMA, 2012. [http://icma.org/en/icma/knowledge_network/documents/kn/Document/304315/AssetBased_Economic_Development_and_Building_Sustainable_Rural_Communties_Part_3_Existing_Infrastruc].

Ready, M. *Asheville: Land of the Sky*. Northridge, Calif.: Western North Carolina Historical Association/Windsor Publications, 1986.

Rebchook, J. "Lower, Upper Downtown: A Tale of Two Office Markets." *Rocky Mountain News*, Mar. 18, 2003.

Reed, J., Sr. Personal interview, Tupelo, Mississippi, 2003.

Research Triangle Park. 2013. [http://www.rtp.org].

"Reviving Small Towns: America the Creative." *The Economist*, December 19, 2006. [http://www.economist.com/node/8450132].

Rittel, H. W. J., and Webber, M. M. "Dilemmas in a General Theory of Planning," *Policy Sciences*, 1973, *4*, 155–169.

Rubin, H. J. *Renewing Hope Within Neighborhoods of Despair: The Community-Based Development Model*. Albany: State University of New York Press, 2000.

Rubin, H. J., and Rubin, I. S. *Community Organizing and Development*. (2nd ed.). Boston: Allyn & Bacon, 1992.

Rural LISC. 2013. [http://www.ruralisc.org].

Rypkema, D. D. *The Economic Benefits of Historic Preservation: A Community Leader's Guide*. Washington, D.C.: National Trust for Historic Preservation, 1994.

Rypkema, D., Cheong, C., and Mason, R. *Measuring Economic Impacts of Historic Preservation*. A Report to the Advisory Council on Historic Preservation, Washington, D.C., November 2011.

Ryser, G. R., and Popovici, R. "The Fiscal Impact of the Congress Avenue Bridge Bat Colony on the City of Austin." Austin, Tx.: Bat Conservation International, 1999.

Safford, S. *Why the Garden Club Couldn't Save Youngstown.* Cambridge, Mass.: Harvard University Press, 2009.

Sampson, R. J. "What 'Community' Supplies." In R. Ferguson and W. T. Dickens (eds.), *Urban Problems and Community Development.* Washington, D.C.: Brookings Institution, 1999.

Scherman, T. "The Music of Democracy: Wynton Marsalis Puts Jazz in Its Place." *American Heritage,* Oct. 1995; reprinted in *Utne Reader,* Mar.–Apr. 1996 (74), pp. 29–36.

Schorr, L. *Common Purpose.* New York: Anchor/Doubleday, 1997.

Schwartz, H. K. "State Tax Credits for Historic Preservation." Washington, D.C.: National Trust for Historic Preservation, March 2013, p. 1.

Scott, E. *"Broadmoor Lives": A New Orleans Neighborhood's Battle to Recover from Hurricane Katrina (A).* Cambridge, Mass.: Harvard Kennedy School, Harvard University, 2008.

Seattle Office of Sustainability and Environment. 2013. [http://www .seattle.gov/environment/].

Seattle Public Utilities. 2013. [http://www.seattle.gov/util/].

Segedy, J. "How Important Is the Quality of Life in Location Decisions and Local Economic Development." In R. D. Bingham and R. Mier (eds.), *Dilemmas of Urban Economic Development.* Thousand Oaks, Calif.: Sage, 1997.

Seidman, K. F. *Coming Home to New Orleans: Neighborhood Rebuilding After Katrina.* New York: Oxford University Press, 2013.

Shekerjian, D. *Uncommon Genius.* New York: Viking/Penquin Books, 1990.

Sullivan, T. *The Road Ahead: Restoring Wisconsin's Workforce Development:* Report to Governor Scott Walker, Madison, Wisconsin, August 2012. [http://doa.wi.gov/secy/documents/sullivanreport .pdf].

Surowiecki, J. *The Wisdom of Crowds.* New York: Anchor/Random House, 2004.

Sustainable Seattle. 2013. [http://www.sustainableseattle.org].

"Taking the Next Step: Tualatin Valley Water District's Journey Toward Sustainability." Beaverton, Oreg.: Tualatin Valley Water District, 2006. [http://www.tvwd.org/media/17617/sustainability_video _handbook.pdf].

Teaford, J. *The Rough Road to Renaissance: Urban Revitalization in America, 1940–1985.* Baltimore: Johns Hopkins Press, 1990.

Thorpe, R. Speech presented to Providence Civic Entrepreneurs, Providence, Rhode Island, 1998.

Tobin, J. *To Conquer the Air: The Wright Brothers and the Great Race for Flight.* New York: Free Press, 2003.

Town of Lake Lure, North Carolina. 2013. [http://www.townof lakelure.com/].

"TriMet Kicks Off Light Rail Bridge Construction." *Metro Magazine,* July 5, 2011. [http://www.metro-magazine.com/news/story /2011/07/trimet-kicks-off-light-rail-bridge-construction.aspx]

"Triple Bottom Line." *The Economist,* November 17, 2009. [http://www .economist.com/node/14301663].

Tupelo, Mississippi. [http://www.ci.tupelo.ms.us].

Turner, M. A. "Adopting a Place-Conscious Approach to Community Development: A Conversation with Margery Austin Turner of the Urban Institute." *Community Dividend,* Federal Reserve Bank of Minneapolis, October 1, 2010. [http://www.minneapolisfed.org /publications_papers/pub_display.cfm?id=4547].

Tyler, N. *Historic Preservation: An Introduction to Its History, Principles, and Practice.* New York: Norton, 2000.

U.S. Bureau of the Census. 2010. [http://uscensus.gov/2010 census/].

U.S. Department of Health and Human Services. (Jan. 7). "Literature Review: Developing a Conceptual Framework to Assess the Sustainability of Community Coalitions Post-Federal Funding." Washington, D.C.: Department of Health and Human Services, 2011. [http://aspe.hhs.gov/health/reports/2010 /sustainlit/].

U.S. Travel Association. "Travel Means Jobs." 2012. [http://www .ustravel.org/sites/default/files/page/2012/08/e-Travel_Means _Jobs-2012.pdf].

Vermont Joint Fiscal Committee. "Pregnancy Care Program to Improve Maternal and Infant Health Outcomes." September 26, 2011. [http://dvha.vermont.gov/budget-legislative/pregnancy -care-program-report-09-26-2011.pdf].

Virginia Department of Historic Resources. 2013. [http://www.dhr .virginia.gov/].

Volkswagen Group of America. News release, July 15, 2008.

Wall Street Journal Online. "Austin Economic Study: Tech Contributes $21B; 150 Tech CEOs Lead National Discussion on Leveraging Innovation Economy." May 6, 2013. [http://online.wsj.com /article/PR-CO-20130506–900854.html].

Watkins, M. "Birminghan Civil Rights District Named Attraction of the Year." *The Birmingham News,* August 30, 2012.

Wausau, Wisconsin. [http://www.ci.wausau.wi.us].

Whitacre, A. "Insiders and Outsiders." The 2013 MIT-Knight Civic Media Conference, April 12, 2013. [http://civic.mit.edu /conference2013].

Williams, M., and Boyle, J. "From Ghost Town to Boom Town." *Asheville Citizen-Times*, Jan. 26, 2003, pp. A1, A5.

Witters, D. "Where You'll Want to Live in 2032." *Gallup Business Journal*, July 10, 2012. [businessjournal.gallup.com /content155510/live-2032.aspx#2].

Yankelovich, D. *Starting with the People*. New York: Houghton Mifflin, 1988.

Index